Houghton Mifflin

Math

- For mathematically promising students
- Opportunities to explore, extend, and connect mathematical ideas

HOUGHTON MIFFLIN BOSTON

A Note to the Teacher

According to the *Principles and Standards for School Mathematics,* "All students need access to a coherent, challenging mathematic curriculum."

In the monograph *Activating Mathematical Talent,* the editors stress "the importance of recognizing and activating promising students' mathematical talent." According to their research, activities that foster critical thinking and reasoning skills meet the following criteria:

- Problems should go beyond routine classroom exercises.
- Problems should be interesting, tantalizing, and engaging.
- Creativity should take precedence over prior knowledge or mathematical training.
- Different approaches to each problem should be tried, discussed, and evaluated.

In order to engage the mathematical talents of all of our students it is necessary to continually provide a variety of activities that allow students to explore, extend, and connect the mathematical concepts and relationships presented in each chapter. Many students will frequently find these Chapter Challenges interesting and supportive of the learning objectives of the chapter.

Some students will consistently turn to Chapter Challenges as a resource for more stimulating problems and a deeper understanding of the mathematics. These so-called "promising mathematical students" will benefit most from Chapter Challenges.

Nevertheless, because we cannot always identify which students will successfully complete a given chapter challenge, it is important to expose *all* students to these more challenging contexts. As a result, Chapter Challenges provides promising mathematical students with consistent exposure to higher-level thinking situations while providing all students access to mathematical enrichments.

Principles and Standards for School Mathematics, (2000) National Council of Teachers of Mathematics.

Vogali, Bruce R. and Alexander Karp, Editors, (2003) *Activating Mathematical Talent,* NCSM Monograph Series, Volume 1.

Contents

Chapter 1 Explore — Use Place Value 1
Chapter 1 Extend — Understanding Scientific Notation 3
Chapter 1 Connect — Investigating Hexadecimals 5

Chapter 2 Explore — Examine Addition Properties 7
Chapter 2 Extend — Using Sumerian Numbers 9
Chapter 2 Connect — Assessing Election Returns 11

Chapter 3 Explore — Operations and Properties 13
Chapter 3 Extend — Applying Multiplication Concepts 15
Chapter 3 Connect — Lattice Multiplication 17

Chapter 4 Explore — Estimate Greater or Less? 19
Chapter 4 Extend — Divide by Doubling 21
Chapter 4 Connect — Math and Test Scores 23

Chapter 5 Explore — Mystery Division 25
Chapter 5 Extend — The Division Algorithm 27
Chapter 5 Connect — Division Choices 29

Chapter 6 Explore — Measuring Volume 31
Chapter 6 Extend — Significant Digits 33
Chapter 6 Connect — Conversions 35

Chapter 7 Explore — Surveys and Double Bar Graphs 37
Chapter 7 Extend — Bar Graphs and Line Graphs 39
Chapter 7 Connect — Misleading Histograms 41

Chapter 8 Explore — Packaging Preferences 43
Chapter 8 Extend — Measures of Greatness 45
Chapter 8 Connect — Agenian Ages 47

Chapter 9 Explore — Identify Prime and Composite Numbers 49
Chapter 9 Extend — Investigating Fractions 51
Chapter 9 Connect — The Stock Market 53

Chapter 10 Explore — Estimation Decisions 55
Chapter 10 Extend — Fraction Number Patterns 57
Chapter 10 Connect — Math and Weather 59

Chapter 11 Explore — Add and Subtract Decimals 61
Chapter 11 Extend — Identify and Correct Errors 63
Chapter 11 Connect — Math and Stock Prices 65

Chapter 12 Explore — Fraction Products 67
Chapter 12 Extend — Use Fractions to Compare 69
Chapter 12 Connect — Fraction Division 71

Contents

Chapter 13 Explore	Relate Multiplication and Division	73
Chapter 13 Extend	Converting Measurements	75
Chapter 13 Connect	Decimal Movement	77
Chapter 14 Explore	Divisor/Quotient Relationships	79
Chapter 14 Extend	Powers of 10	81
Chapter 14 Connect	Decimal Division	83
Chapter 15 Explore	Investigate Points and Lines	85
Chapter 15 Extend	The Pythagorean Theorem	87
Chapter 15 Connect	Analyze a Street Map	89
Chapter 16 Explore	Investigate Perimeter	91
Chapter 16 Extend	Estimate Area	93
Chapter 16 Connect	Planetary Circumferences	95
Chapter 17 Explore	Triangular Pyramids	97
Chapter 17 Extend	Nets	99
Chapter 17 Connect	Area and Volume	101
Chapter 18 Explore	Ratios in the Garden	103
Chapter 18 Extend	Rates	105
Chapter 18 Connect	Estimating Distances on a Map	107
Chapter 19 Explore	Determining Percents	109
Chapter 19 Extend	Use Percents	111
Chapter 19 Connect	People Percentages	113
Chapter 20 Explore	Combinations	115
Chapter 20 Extend	Probability at Play	117
Chapter 20 Connect	The Weather	119
Chapter 21 Explore	Equations as Clues	121
Chapter 21 Extend	Price Reductions and Increased Sales	123
Chapter 21 Connect	The Cost of a Music CD	125
Chapter 22 Explore	Integers and the Motion of a Spring	127
Chapter 22 Extend	Integer Cubes	129
Chapter 22 Connect	Integer Puzzles	131
Chapter 23 Explore	Using Ordered Pairs in the Coordinate Plane	133
Chapter 23 Extend	Graphing Linear Functions	135
Chapter 23 Connect	Transformations in the Coordinate Plane	137

Name ______________________ Date __________

Use Place Value

Imagine you are the inventor of the largest cash machine in the world. Your machine dispenses money in amounts up to hundreds of thousands of dollars. Bank customers can tell the machine the denomination of bills they want to receive. Before you can install the machine, though, you need to finish programming it.

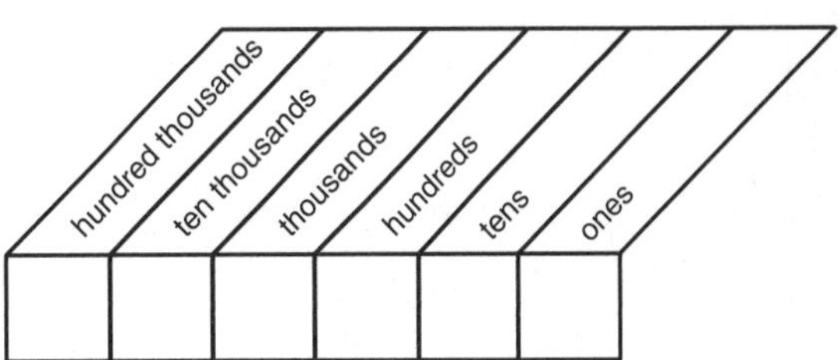

1. Use the place-value chart above to answer **a–c.**

a. Start at the tens place and move one place to the left. What is the value of this place compared to your starting place? ______________________

b. Start at the tens place and move three places to the left. What is the value of this place compared to your starting place? ______________________

c. Start at the hundred thousands place and move four places to the right. What is the value of this place compared to your starting place? __________

2. Analyze Describe the relationship between movement on the place–value chart and the place value of digits.

____

Now use the place-value chart for Exercises 3 and 4 to finish programming your machine.

3. If a customer asks for $10,000 in $10 bills, how many bills will the machine dispense? __________ if the customer asks for $1,000? __________

4. If a customer asks for $100,000 in $10 bills, how many bills will the machine dispense? _____ if the customer asks for $1,000? _____

Explore It

Can you use the place-value chart to handle a customer's request for $200,000 in $100 bills? Explain your answer.

Teacher Notes

Explore: Use Place Value

Objective Explore place-value relationships.

Using the Explore (Activities to use after Lesson 1)

An understanding of place value and the base-ten system underlies almost all mathematical exploration. In this activity, students explore the relationship between place values up to hundred thousands and identify how they can navigate from place to place using powers of ten. The Explore It encourages students to apply this relationship to other numbers.

Math Journal You may wish to have students use their *Math Journals* for the Explore It.

Going Beyond Encourage students to extend the place-value chart to the left by continuing to multiply the highest place value by ten. As the place values increase, students can either identify them by their conventional names or create their own names for the places.

Solutions

1. **a.** It is 10 times greater.

   b. It is 1,000 times greater.

   c. It is 10,000 times less.

2. *Answers may vary. Sample:* As you move to the left, each place is 10 times greater. As you move to the right, each place is 10 times less.

3. 1,000; 10

4. 10,000; 100

Explore It *Answers may vary. Sample:* Yes. I would write a 2 to remind me that the customer is asking for $200,000 instead of $100,000. Then I would start at the hundreds place and move three places to the left to get to the hundred thousands place. This place is 1,000 times greater than my starting point, so I multiply 2 by 1,000 to get an answer of 2 thousand $100 bills.

Name ______________________ Date ____________

Understanding Scientific Notation

A number written in scientific notation has two factors. One factor is greater than or equal to 1 but less than 10. The other factor is a power of 10.

Here is how to write 865,000 using scientific notation.

- Place a decimal point to the right of the ones place. — 865,000.
- Move the decimal point to the left to make a number greater than or equal to 1 but less than 10. — 8.65,000.
- Write the number of decimal places moved as the exponent in the power of 10. — 10^5
- Drop any zeros to the right of the decimal point. — 8.65
- Write the new number multiplied by the power of 10. — 8.65×10^5

So $865{,}000 = 8.65 \times 10^5$

Write each number using scientific notation.

1. Distance in miles between the Earth and the moon: 239,000 ____________
2. Meters that light travels in a second: 300,000,000 ____________
3. Hours in a day on Pluto: 153 ____________
4. Number of water molecules in a liter of water: 33,000,000,000,000,000,000,000,000

   ____

5. **Compare** Which is greater: 2.6×10^7 or 8.93×10^4? Why? ____________

   ____

   ____

Extend It

What generalizations can you make about when it is helpful to write numbers in scientific notation? Write a paragraph explaining your generalizations.

Teacher Notes

Extend: Understanding Scientific Notation

Objective Use scientific notation to explore decimals and the relationship between place value and exponents.

Using the Extend (Activities to use after Lesson 3)

In this activity, students use scientific notation to extend their knowledge of decimals, place value, and exponents. Real-world examples of scientific notation introduce students to the concept. Writing numbers in standard form and using scientific notation gives students the opportunity to apply their decimal and place value skills. In the Extend It, students use their experience with scientific notation to analyze its usefulness.

Math Journal You may wish to have students use their *Math Journals* for the Extend It.

Going Beyond Have students look for examples of scientific notation or large numbers in standard form in articles and books. Ask students to change the numbers they find from one form to another.

Solutions

1. 2.39×10^5
2. 3×10^8
3. 1.53×10^2
4. 3.3×10^{25}
5. 2.6×10^7
   Explanations may vary. Sample: Ten to the seventh power means the number is in the ten millions place. Ten to the fourth power means the number is only in the ten thousands place.

Extend It *Answers may vary. Sample:* Scientific notation is useful for writing greater numbers because you do not have to write as many zeros.

Name ______________________ Date ____________

Investigating Hexadecimals

The hexadecimal system is a base-sixteen number system. Each place in a hexadecimal place-value chart has a value from 0 to 15. Letters are used to represent values 10 through 15. For example, the base-ten number 13 is written as the hexadecimal number D.

Base Ten	0	1	2	3	4	5	6	7	8	9	10	11	12	**13**	14	15
Hexadecimal	0	1	2	3	4	5	6	7	8	9	A	B	C	**D**	E	F

The base-ten number 24 is written as the hexadecimal number 18.

The base-ten number 43 is written as the hexadecimal number 2B.

Sixteens	Ones
1	8

$24 = (1 \times 16) + (8 \times 1)$

Sixteens	Ones
2	B

$43 = (2 \times 16) + (11 \times 1)$

Complete to find the hexadecimal number for each base-ten number given.

1. 19

Base Ten

Tens	Ones

___ = (___ × 10) + (___ × 1)

Hexadecimal

Sixteens	Ones

___ = (___ × 16) + (___ × 1)

2. 28

Base Ten

Tens	Ones

___ = (___ × 10) + (___ × 1)

Hexadecimal

Sixteens	Ones

___ = (___ × 16) + (___ × 1)

3. Decide Is the base-ten number 222 equal to the hexadecimal number 222? Explain.

____

Connect It

Which number system is easier to use, base ten or hexadecimal? Write a paragraph comparing the two number systems.

Teacher Notes

Connect: Investigating Hexadecimals

Objective Use the hexadecimal number system to investigate place value.

Using the Connect (Activities to use after Lesson 5)

This activity encourages students to compare the familiar base-ten place-value chart with another method of counting and creating numbers. Hexadecimal, or base-sixteen, numbers are used to represent numbers in Internet design and some aspects of computer programming. Students use base-ten and hexadecimal place value to write equivalent values in each number system. Students are encouraged to use expanded notation to analyze how place value is used to represent numbers. The Connect It asks students to analyze the strengths and weaknesses of each number system.

Math Journal You may wish to have students use their *Math Journals* to answer the Connect It question.

Going Beyond RGB codes use hexadecimal numbers to tell a computer what combination of red, green, and blue lights to display on a computer monitor. Have students research these codes and learn what they represent. Have students identify the codes for black, white, red, blue, green, and other colors.

Solutions

1.

Base Ten

Tens	Ones
1	9

19 = (1 × 10) + (9 × 1)

Hexadecimal

Sixteens	Ones
1	3

19 = (1 × 16) + (3 × 1)

2.

Base Ten

Tens	Ones
2	8

28 = (2 × 10) + (8 × 1)

Hexadecimal

Sixteens	Ones
1	C

28 = (1 × 16) + (12 × 1)

3. No; *Explanations may vary. Sample:* The hexadecimal number 222 equals the base-ten number 546.

Connect It *Answers may vary. Sample:* The base-ten system is easier to use because it is easier to group and multiply values of ten. In the hexadecimal system, the mix of numbers and letters is confusing. One advantage that the hexadecimal system has is that you can include greater number values in fewer places than you can in the base-ten system.

Name ______________________ Date ____________

Examine Addition Properties

Do you think the Commutative, Associative, and Identity Properties of Addition hold true for subtraction? You can use expressions to find out.

Apply the Commutative Property to this expression.

$8 + n =$ ____ $+$ ____

Assign a value for n and solve the equation. Let $n = 6$.

$8 +$ ____ $=$ ____ $+$ ____

____ $=$ ____

Are both sides of the equation equal?

____

Now rewrite the expression using subtraction.

$8 - n \stackrel{?}{=}$ ____ $-$ ____

Let $n = 6$.

$8 -$ ____ $\stackrel{?}{=}$ ____ $-$ ____

____ $\stackrel{?}{=}$ ____

Are both sides of the equation equal?

____

1. **Infer** What conclusion can you make about the Commutative Property and subtraction? ____________________

2. **Generalize** How can you determine whether the Associative and Identity Properties of addition also apply to subtraction? ____________________

Use the following examples to determine whether the given property applies to subtraction. Let $x = 2$. Write <u>yes</u> or <u>no</u> to tell whether the property applies to subtraction.

3. Associative Property
   $10 + (7 + x)$ ____________

4. Identity Property
   $x + 0$ ____________

Explore It

What can you tell about the importance of the order of numbers in addition and subtraction? Explain your answer.

Teacher Notes

Explore: Examine Addition Properties

Objective Use algebraic expressions to explore addition properties and determine whether the properties apply to subtraction.

Using the Explore (Activities to use after Lesson 1)

Students have learned the Commutative, Associative, and Identity properties of addition. In this activity, students learn about the significance of these properties by attempting to apply them to subtraction. In the Explore It students summarize their results by comparing the importance of number order in addition and subtraction.

Math Journal You may wish to have students use their *Math Journals* to answer the Explore It question.

Going Beyond Have students investigate multiplication properties, including the Commutative Property, the Associative Property, and the Identity Property. Ask them to compare these properties to the addition properties and to note similarities and differences between the property sets.

Solutions

$8 + n = n + 8$
$8 + 6 = 6 + 8$
$14 = 14$
Yes.

$8 - n \stackrel{?}{=} n - 8$
$8 - 6 \stackrel{?}{=} 6 - 8$
$2 \neq {}^{-}2$
No. Not all students will answer ${}^{-}2$, but they should recognize that $6 - 8 \neq 2$. So the answer is still no.

1. *Answers may vary. Sample:* The Commutative Property does not apply to subtraction.
2. *Answers may vary. Sample:* You can apply each property to different subtraction examples and see if the properties hold true.
3. $10 + (7 + 2) = (10 + 7) + 2$
   $10 + 9 = 17 + 2$
   $19 = 19$

   $10 - (7 - 2) \stackrel{?}{=} (10 - 7) - 2$
   $10 - 5 \stackrel{?}{=} 3 - 2$
   $5 \neq 1$
   No. The Associative Property does not apply to subtraction.
4. $2 + 0 = 2$
   $2 = 2$
   $2 - 0 \stackrel{?}{=} 2$
   $2 = 2$
   Yes. The Identity Property applies to subtraction.

Explore It *Answers may vary. Sample:* When you are adding numbers, the order of the numbers is not important. When you subtract, the order of the numbers is very important.

Name ______________________ Date __________

Using Sumerian Numbers

The Roman number system existed before our number system. They wrote their numbers using combinations of letters. Thousands of years before the Romans, the ancient Sumerians used a different number system. They used these six symbols to represent their numbers.

D	○	▽	▽ with ○	◯	◎
1	10	60	600	3,600	36,000

Use the Sumerian number symbols to add and subtract. Write each number below the Sumerian number symbols. Draw the Sumerian number symbols for each sum or difference.

1. ○○ DDD + ▽ DD =

   ______ + ______ = ______

2. ▽ ○ DDDD − ○ D =

   ______ − ______ = ______

3. ▽(○) ○ DD − ▽▽▽▽▽ ○○○○ DDDD =

   ______ − ______ = ______

4. ◯ + ▽(○) ▽(○) ▽ =

   ______ + ______ = ______

5. **Analyze** Look at the Sumerian symbols you drew for the sums in Exercises 1 and 4. Explain how these symbols relate to the symbols used for the addends in these exercises.

   ____

   ____

Extend It

Do you think that the people of ancient Sumeria often used numbers such as 2,145,919? Explain why or why not.

Teacher Notes

Extend: Using Sumerian Numbers

Objective Extend addition and subtraction skills by using the ancient Sumerian number system.

Using the Extend (Activities to use after Lesson 3)

The Sumerian number system is one of the earliest known number systems, dating back to the third millenium BCE. It consists of six symbols, which are used to represent numbers in a simple accumulative fashion. In this activity, students decipher numbers written in Sumerian form and solve equations with them. Students are encouraged to come up with their own problem-solving strategies. In the Extend It students consider the advantages and limitations of the Sumerian number system.

Math Journal You may wish to have students use their *Math Journals* to answer the Extend It question.

Going Beyond Have students research other ancient number systems and compare them to the Sumerian system. Have them assess whether adding and subtracting is easier or more difficult using the other number systems.

Solutions

1. 23 + 62 = 85

2. 74 − 11 = 63

3. 612 − 344 = 268

4. 3,600 + 1,260 = 4,860

5. *Answers may vary. Sample:* The symbols used in the sums are a combination of the symbols used in the addends.

Extend It *Answers may vary. Sample:* The Sumerian people probably did not often use numbers such as 2,145,919 because the greatest symbol in their number system was 36,000. If the Sumerians used their symbols to write a number in the millions, it would be very difficult to keep track of the number of symbols.

Name ______________________ Date __________

Assessing Election Returns

It's election night and the results are coming in! You've been placed in charge of calculating vote totals for the elections for the governor and U.S. senator of one state. Here are the results as of 11:00 P.M., three hours after the polls close.

Gubernatorial Race	
Leticia Harmon	1,263,807
Gordon Carrera	948,844
Ellie McGregor	72,432

Senatorial Race	
Elliot Chavis	1,140,594
Patrick Stapleton	1,054,933

1. How many votes separate Leticia Harmon and Gordon Carrera in the race for governor?

____

2. How many votes have been cast in the race for senator? __________

The tally of the remaining votes cast in the election is completed at 10:00 A.M. the next morning. At that time, you learn that each candidate has the number of votes shown at right to add to the previous tally.

Gubernatorial Race	
Leticia Harmon	392,586
Gordon Carrera	683,112
Ellie McGregor	42,729

Senatorial Race	
Elliot Chavis	477,088
Patrick Stapleton	611,950

3. List the total number of votes for each of the candidates:

Leticia Harmon ______________________

Gordon Carrera ______________________

Ellie McGregor ______________________

4. Compare Which number is greater, the number of votes cast for Ellie McGregor or the margin of victory in the governor's race? ______________________

5. Analyze When the first results came in on election night, Patrick Stapleton stated that he needs more than half of the votes remaining to be counted for a victory. Using estimation, do you think he was right? How can you tell? ______________________

Connect It

Suppose the results of the governor's race were different and Gordon Carrera won the election. Describe two different ways the votes for each candidate could have been cast.

Teacher Notes

Connect: Assessing Election Returns

Objective Add and subtract greater numbers to determine the final results of a statewide election.

Using the Connect (Activities to use after Lesson 5)
Election returns are one of the most prominent examples of the real-world addition and subtraction of greater numbers. In this activity, students analyze the results of fictitious statewide elections for governor and senator. The problems require them to add and subtract greater numbers for the purpose of determining vote totals and differentials. In the Connect It, students assess the types of possible vote changes that could alter the election results.

Math Journal You may wish to have students use their *Math Journals* to answer the Connect It question.

Going Beyond Have students look up actual state or national election results in an almanac or other source. Have them analyze the numbers they find to determine the margin of victory and the total number of votes cast.

Solutions

1. 314,963 votes
2. 2,195,527 votes
3. Leticia Harmon: 1,656,393 votes; Gordon Carrera: 1,631,956 votes; Ellie McGregor: 115,161 votes.
4. The total number of votes cast for Ellie McGregor: 115,161 > 24,437.
5. Yes. I think he was right. *Answers may vary. Sample:* At 11 P.M. Stapleton is down about 100,000 votes. About 1,000,000 votes remain to be counted. 100,000 for Stapleton from 1,000,000 would tie the candidates. Stapleton would need about 500,000 of the remaining 900,000 to win. So, 100,000 + 500,000 = 600,000. 600,000 is more than half 1,000,000.

Connect It *Answers may vary. Sample:* The votes could have been cast this way: Leticia Harmon: 1,656,393; Gordon Carrera: 1,656,394; Ellie McGregor: 90,723. Leticia Harmon had won by 24,437 votes. In order for Gordon Carrera to win, he would have to receive 24,438 of Ellie McGregor's votes.

The votes could be cast another way. 10,000 from Leticia Harmon's total and 10,000 from Ellie McGregor's total is 20,000 votes added to Gordon Carrera's total. The final would be Harmon 1,646,393; McGregor 105,161; Carrera 1,651,956.

Name ____________________ Date __________

Operations and Properties

You learned about the Associative, Commutative, Identity, and Zero properties of multiplication. You can use expressions to find out whether the properties apply to division.

Write a multiplication expression and apply the Commutative Property.

$6 \times n =$ _____ $\times$ _____

Assign a value for n, and then solve the equation. Let $n = 2$.

$6 \times$ _____ $=$ _____ $\times$ _____

$12 =$ _____

Are the expressions on both sides of the equation equal? __________

Now rewrite the expression and replace the operation of multiplication with division.

$6 \div n =$ _____ $\div$ _____

Let $n = 2$.

$6 \div$ _____ $\stackrel{?}{=}$ _____ $\div$ _____

_____ $\stackrel{?}{=}$ _____

Are the expressions on both sides of the equation equal? __________

1. **Infer** What conclusion can you make about the Commutative Property and division?

   Support your conclusion with another example. ____________________

   ____

2. **Generalize** How do you think you can determine if the Associative, Identity, and Zero properties of multiplication apply to division?

   ____

Use the following examples to determine if each property applies to division. Write <u>yes</u> or <u>no</u>. Let $a = 2$.

3. Associative Property

   $20 \times (4 \times a)$ __________

4. Identity Property

   $1 \times a$ __________

5. Zero Property

   $a \times 0$ __________

Explore It

When does the Identity Property apply to division?
When does the Zero Property apply to division? Explain.

Teacher Notes

Explore: Operations and Properties

Objective Use algebraic expressions to explore multiplication properties and determine whether the properties apply to division.

Using the Explore (Activities to use after Lesson 1)

Students may not always realize that properties are specific to operations. This activity requires students to use algebraic expressions to explore the application of multiplication properties to division. The Explore It encourages students to use the Commutative Property to determine in which cases the Identity and Zero Properties apply to division.

Math Journal You may wish to have students use their *Math Journals* to answer the Explore It question.

Going Beyond Have students create and solve a word problem in which they evaluate the expression $5 \times (4 \times a)$ for $a = 6$, and apply the Associative Property. *Sample problem:* There are 5 parking areas. Each car in the parking area has 4 tires. How many tires are there in all if there are 6 cars in each parking area? Solution: $5 \times (4 \times 6) = (5 \times 4) \times 6 = 20 \times 6 = 120$ tires.

Solutions

$6 \times n = n \times 6$
$6 \times 2 = 2 \times 6$
$12 = 12$
Yes.

$6 \div n \stackrel{?}{=} n \div 6$
$6 \div 2 \stackrel{?}{=} 2 \div 6$
$3 \neq \frac{1}{3}$
No.

1. *Answers may vary. Sample:* The Commutative Property does not apply to division. Example: $15 \div 5 = 3; 5 \div 15 = \frac{1}{3}; 3 \neq \frac{1}{3}$.
2. *Answers may vary. Sample:* You can apply each property to different division examples and see if the properties hold true.
3. $20 \times (4 \times 2) = (20 \times 4) \times 2$
   $20 \times 8 = 80 \times 2$
   $160 = 160$
   $20 \div (4 \div 2) \stackrel{?}{=} (20 \div 4) \div 2$
   $20 \div 2 \stackrel{?}{=} 5 \div 2$
   $10 \neq 2\frac{1}{2}$

   No. The Associative Property does not apply to division.
4. $1 \times 2 = 2; 1 \div 2 \stackrel{?}{=} 2; \frac{1}{2} \neq 2$

   No. The Identity Property does not apply to division in this case.
5. $2 \times 0 = 0; 2 \div 0 \stackrel{?}{=}$ undefined

   No. You cannot divide by zero. The Zero Property does not apply to division in this case.

Explore It *Answers may vary. Sample:* When you divide by 1 the Identity Property applies to division. The quotient of any number divided by 1 is that number. When you divide zero by any number the Zero Property applies to division. The quotient of zero divided by any number is zero.

Name ______________________ Date __________

Applying Multiplication Concepts

Imagine taking a jet to school! Sound impossible? Well, you may not be taking a jet to school, but in the near future, private jets could replace cars. The chart shows data about current aircraft and the NASA jet of the future. NASA is working with industry and colleges on projects like this.

Use a separate sheet of paper to answer the questions.

Different Aircraft		
Aircraft	**No. of passengers**	**Speed**
Boeing 747	524	576 mph
Cessna 337	4	190 mph
NASA jet of the future	2–10	600 mph

1. **Decide** Use the data to decide which jet listed in the chart you would take in each of the following types of trip. Explain your choice in each case.

	Trip Information			
	Type of Trip	**Departure Time**	**Latest Time of Arrival**	**Distance**
a.	Business	9:00 A.M.	5:00 P.M.	2,000 miles
b.	Business	7:30 A.M.	8:30 A.M.	400 miles
c.	Pleasure	4:00 P.M.	No set time	400 miles

2. **Compare** A Cessna 337 holds about 93 gallons of fuel. The NASA jet will hold about 1,373 gallons of fuel. If a gallon of fuel weighs a little less than 7 pounds, about how many more pounds of fuel does the NASA jet hold than the Cessna 337? What advantage might this give to NASA's jet? What disadvantage?

3. **Analyze** Which operation did you use to answer Question 2? Why?

4. The NASA jet descends at a rate of 2,124 feet per minute. After several minutes the plane lands. What information do you need to determine the altitude of the airplane when it started its descent? Why?

Extend It

Suppose a passenger traveled 2 hours on one plane listed in the Different Aircraft chart above and 3 hours on another plane for a total distance of 2,928 miles. Which two planes has the passenger traveled on?

Teacher Notes

Extend: Applying Multiplication Concepts

Objective Use multiplication to analyze and interpret data about air transportation.

Using the Extend (Activities to use after Lesson 4)

In this activity, students use critical thinking to analyze a chart and explore and compare a jet of the future with aircraft typically used today in commercial transportation. The Extend It is a non-routine problem in which students can apply a guess-and-check problem-solving strategy.

Math Journal You may wish to have students use their *Math Journals* to answer the questions on the Extend page.

Going Beyond Have students research other types of aircraft used commercially and compare them to the jet of the future being studied by NASA. Encourage students to analyze advantages and disadvantages of each.

Solutions

1. *Answers may vary. Sample:*
   a. 747; because you can arrive within 4 hours, and because the plane holds more people it is probably bigger and there is more room to work while you fly.
   b. NASA jet; because it is smaller, you board more quickly, and it still travels 400 miles in less than 1 hour.
   c. Cessna; there is no set time to arrive, so you can take a slower plane.
2. The Cessna holds about $7 \times 93 = 651$ pounds of fuel, while the NASA jet will hold about $7 \times 1{,}373 = 9{,}611$ pounds of fuel. The NASA jet holds about 9,000 more pounds of fuel than the Cessna 337.

   Answers may vary. Sample: An advantage of the NASA jet is that it will be able to fly a longer distance because it can hold more fuel. A disadvantage is that it would have to carry more weight.
3. Multiplication; because you know that 1 gallon of fuel weighs a little less than 7 pounds and you want to find out how much 93 gallons of fuel and 1,373 gallons of fuel weigh.
4. You need to know how many minutes it took for the plane to descend. Then you could multiply the number of minutes by the rate per minute to find out the altitude of the plane when it started its descent.

Extend It The passenger traveled 3 hours on the Boeing 747 and 2 hours on the NASA jet.

Name ______________________ Date __________

Lattice Multiplication

Lattice multiplication was introduced in Europe by the mathematician Fibonacci during the 1200s. Look at how to use this method to multiply: 358 × 26.

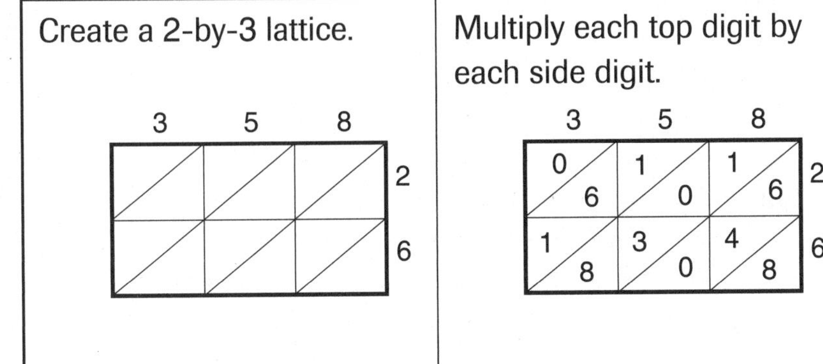

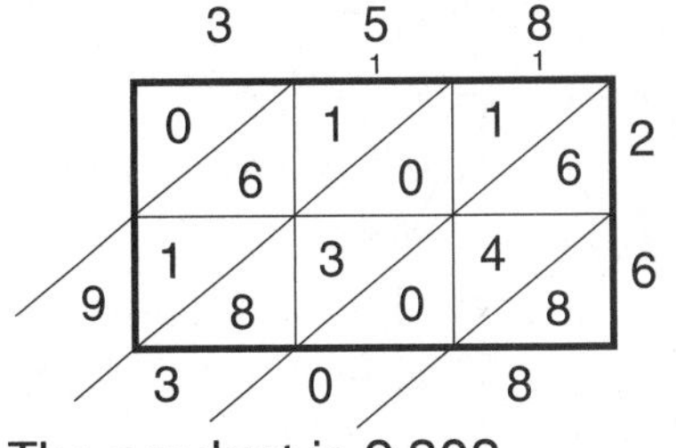

On a separate sheet of paper, use lattice multiplication to find each product.

1. 45 × 56 **2.** 156 × 12 **3.** 427 × 73

4. Compare and Contrast How is lattice multiplication the same as the traditional method you learned? How is it different?

____

5. Hypothesize Which multiplication property is the basis for the lattice method of multiplication? ______________________________

6. Summarize Use what you know about the traditional method of two-digit multiplication and lattice multiplication to explain which method you prefer and why.

____

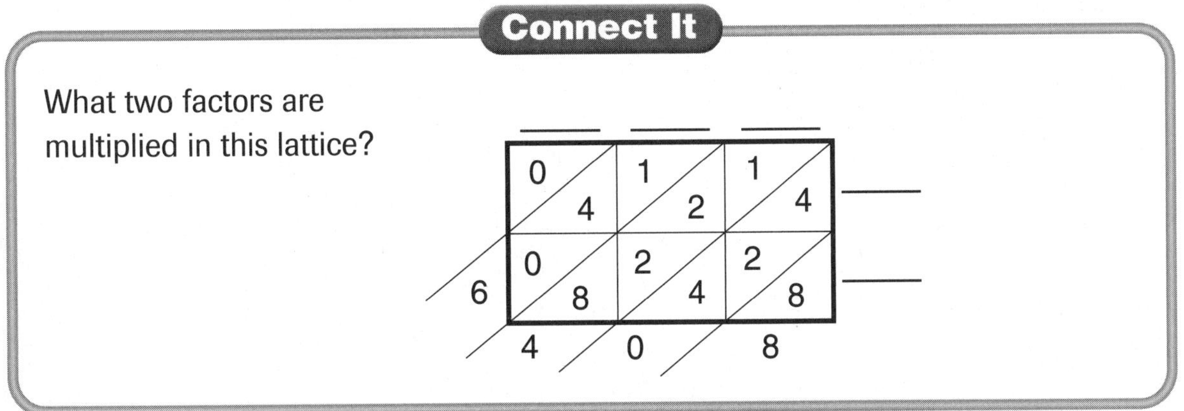

Teacher Notes

Connect: Lattice Multiplication

Objective Multiply two-digit numbers using the lattice multiplication method.

Using the Connect (Activities to use after Lesson 5)

This activity demonstrates the lattice method of multiplication. The questions encourage students to connect what they know about multiplication with this alternative method. Students discover that both methods involve multiplication, regrouping, and addition, but in a different order. The Connect It helps students use logical reasoning to identify the two factors that are multiplied in a completed lattice.

Math Journal You may wish to have students use their *Math Journals* to answer Exercises 1–3 and the Connect It question.

Going Beyond Have students research the Russian Peasant Multiplication Algorithm. In this algorithm students halve the factor in column 1 as they double the factor in column 2. Continue until the number in column 1 becomes 1. For example, for 12×27:

Halves	Doubles
12	27
6	54
3	108
1	216

When halving odd numbers drop the remainder. Add the numbers in the doubles column corresponding to odd numbers in the halves column: $108 + 216 = 324$. So, $12 \times 27 = 324$.

Solutions

1\.

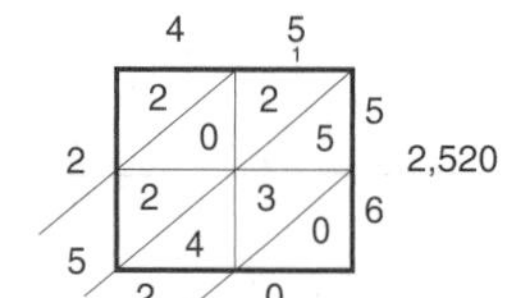

2\.

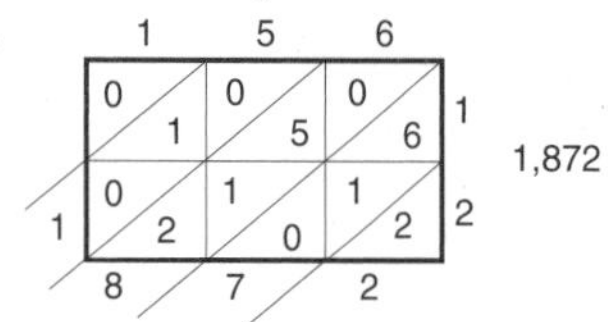

3\.

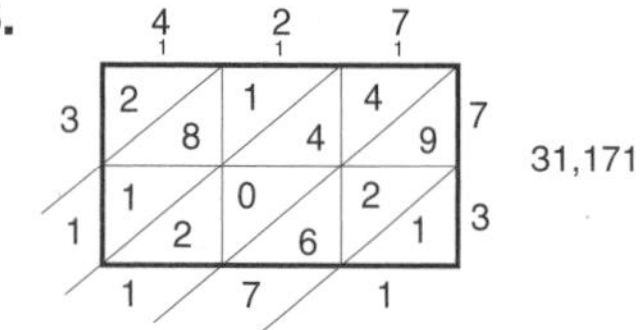

4\. *Answers may vary. Sample:* They are the same because in both methods you multiply, regroup, and add. They are different because you do the operations in a different order.

5\. Distributive Property

6\. *Answers may vary. Sample:* I prefer lattice multiplication because when you multiply you do not have to regroup numbers. You regroup when you add and I think that is easier.

Connect It 267×24

Name ______________________ Date __________

Estimate Greater or Less?

When you use compatible numbers to estimate a quotient, sometimes your estimate is greater or less than the actual quotient. The compatible numbers you choose can help you decide if the estimate is greater or less.

Estimate 415 ÷ 6.	Estimate 315 ÷ 6.
• Increase the dividend to estimate. 420 ÷ 6 = 70	• Decrease the dividend to estimate. 300 ÷ 6 = 50
• Use a calculator to find the actual quotient. 415 ÷ 6 = _____	• Use a calculator to find the actual quotient. 315 ÷ 6 = _____
The estimate is _____ than the actual quotient.	The estimate is _____ than the actual quotient.

Estimate. Decide if the actual quotient is greater or less than the estimate.

1. 5,217 ÷ 6

5,400 ÷ 6 = _____

The estimate is _____ than the actual quotient.

2. 12,078 ÷ 5

10,000 ÷ 5 = _____

The estimate is _____ than the actual quotient.

3. 71,076 ÷ 9

72,000 ÷ 9 = _____

The estimate is _____ than the actual quotient.

4. Explain How can you use compatible numbers to estimate 14,765 ÷ 7 so that the estimate is greater than the actual quotient? How can you use compatible numbers so that the estimate is less than the actual quotient?

____

5. Timmy has $37. He plans to order CDs on the Internet. They cost $8 each. Should he estimate an amount greater or less than the exact number he can order? Explain. Why should he do this?

____

Explore It

Describe a situation where an estimate should be greater than the exact quotient, and another in which the estimate should be less than the exact quotient.

Teacher Notes

Explore: Estimate Greater or Less?

Objective Determine if an estimate will be more or less than the actual quotient.

Using the Explore (Activities to use after Lesson 1)

This activity provides the opportunity for students to make logical decisions about how and when to overestimate or underestimate a quotient. The Explore It encourages students to create original situations for each type of estimate.

Math Journal You may wish to have students use their *Math Journals* to answer the Explore It.

Going Beyond Present the following situation to students: You need to drive a distance of 680 miles over the next 7 days, and want to drive about the same number of miles each day. Have students explain the advantage or disadvantage of making an overestimate of the number of miles they should drive each day. Students should realize it is better to overestimate so that they are sure to drive the distance needed.

Solutions

$415 \div 6 = 69.17$
The estimate is greater than the actual quotient.

$315 \div 6 = 52.5$
The estimate is less than the actual quotient.

1. 900; The estimate is greater than the actual quotient.
2. 2,000; The estimate is less than the actual quotient.
3. 8,000; The estimate is greater than the actual quotient.
4. *Answers may vary. Sample:* Increase the dividend to 21,000 and estimate $21{,}000 \div 7 = 3{,}000$. Decrease the dividend to 14,000 and estimate $14{,}000 \div 7 = 2{,}000$.
5. *Answers may vary. Sample:* He should estimate an amount less than the exact number, for example, $\$32 \div 8 = 4$ CDs. If he estimates an amount greater than the exact quotient, he will order more CDs than he can afford. If he estimates less, he can be sure he has enough money.

Explore It *Answers may vary. Sample:* Greater Estimate: Notebooks cost 3 for $5. Estimate the cost of 1 notebook to determine if you have enough money to buy one. Lesser Estimate: If you have $28, how many $9 books can you buy?

Name ______________________ Date __________

Divide by Doubling

Ancient Egyptians used doubling to divide. This method works when dividing numbers that divide evenly. Here is how to divide 95 by 5 using this method.

Make two columns of numbers. Let the first column start with 1. Let the second column start with the divisor. Double each number. Stop when the number in the second column will be greater than 95, the dividend, when doubled.	Look for a combination of numbers in the second column that adds up to 95, the dividend.	Add the numbers in the first column that are paired with the checked numbers that add up to 95.
1 | 5 2 | 10 4 | 20 8 | 40 16 | 80 Stop!	1 | 5✓ 2 | 10✓ 4 | 20 8 | 40 16 | 80✓	1 ← 5✓ 2 ← 10✓ 4 | 20 8 | 40 16 ← 80✓
80 doubled is 160, so Stop!	5 + 10 + 80 = 95	1 + 2 + 16 = _____ 95 ÷ 5 = _____

Use doubling to find each quotient.

1. 76 ÷ 4 = _____

2. 84 ÷ 6 = _____

3. 128 ÷ 8 = _____

4. Compare and Contrast How is the doubling method of division the same as the method you learned in Chapter 4? How is it different?

____

Extend It

Imagine you invented a machine that uses doubling to divide. Explain how the machine works to find 42 ÷ 3.

Teacher Notes

Extend: Divide by Doubling

Objective Learn how to divide by 1-digit numbers using doubling.

Using the Extend (Activities to use after Lesson 3)

The basic method of division as taught in Chapter 4 is only one method of division. In this activity, the ancient Egyptian method using doubling to divide is demonstrated. Although the Egyptians provided a method for dividing numbers that divide evenly as well as for those that do not, only those that divide evenly are presented here. The questions that follow encourage students to compare this method to the one they learned in Chapter 4, and to analyze the operations involved in using this method. The Extend It challenges students to describe the doubling method in their own words.

Math Journal You may wish to have students use their *Math Journals* to answer the Extend It.

Going Beyond Have students use the doubling method to solve a 2-digit division problem similar to the following: 180 ÷ 15. (12)

Solutions

1. 76 ÷ 4 = 19

1 4✓
2 8✓
4 16
8 32
16 64✓
1 + 2 + 16 = 19

2. 84 ÷ 6 = 14

1 6
2 12✓
4 24✓
8 48✓
2 + 4 + 8 = 14

3. 136 ÷ 8 = 17

1 8✓
2 16
4 32
8 64
16 128✓
1 + 16 = 17

4. *Answers may vary. Sample:* You need to use addition or multiplication in both; in doubling you do not need to divide by the divisor.

Extend It *Answers may vary. Sample:* You put in the 42 and 3. The machine doubles 1 on its left side and 3 on its right until doubling 3 reaches 42. Then the machine adds the doubled numbers on its right side whose sum is 42 (6, 12, 24). Finally, it adds the numbers on its left side that match these (2, 4, 8).

Name ______________________ Date __________

Math and Test Scores

Juan's last four test scores in science and math are shown on the right. Juan is hoping to earn a 90 average or above in each subject.

Juan's Test Scores	
Science Tests	**Math Tests**
Test 1: 86	Test 1: 93
Test 2: 91	Test 2: 90
Test 3: 83	Test 3: 87
Test 4: 92	Test 4: 95
Test 5:	Test 5:

Answer each question. Use a calculator.

1. If the variable *n* represents the score on Juan's fifth math test, what equation can you use to represent an average of 90 in math?

   ____

2. What is the lowest score Juan can achieve on the next math test to have at least a 90 average in math? ______________________

3. **Compare** How does the score Juan must get on his next math test compare to the score he must get on his next science test in order to have a 90 average or above in each subject?

   ____

   ____

4. **Predict** Suppose Juan has more science tests before the end of the marking period. What are two possible scores he can earn on the tests and get a 90 average in science?

   ____

5. **Hypothesize** Juan achieves a final average of 92 in math. What score did Juan get on Test 5 in math? Explain how you know. ______________________

   ____

   ____

Connect It

How do the number of tests Juan has left to take in each subject affect calculating the final average?

Teacher Notes

Connect: Math and Test Scores

Objective Solve real-life, multi-step word problems using division.
Materials calculator

Using the Connect (Activities to use after Lesson 5)

In this activity, students use data about test scores in two major subjects to solve multi-step word problems. The problems require students to use what they have learned about division and logical thinking to analyze and predict scores needed to attain a specific average.

Math Journal You may wish to have students use their *Math Journals* to answer the Connect It question.

Going Beyond Provide students with two to three sets of test scores similar to the ones on the student worksheet. Have students use the test scores to write and solve word problems.

Solutions

1. $(93 + 90 + 87 + 95 + n) \div 5 = 90$
2. 85
3. He needs at least 13 points more on his science test than on his math test. He needs a 98 on his science test to get a 90 average, but only an 85 on his math test.
4. *Answers may vary. Sample:* He can get 94 on each test and still get a 90 average.
5. *Answers may vary. Sample:* To get an average of 92, the sum of the test scores had to be 460. The sum of the first 4 scores was 365. $460 - 365 = 95$, so he had to get a 95 to get an average of 92 in math.

Connect It *Answers may vary. Sample:* Each time he takes another test he has to divide the sum of the test scores by a different number to calculate the average. He has to divide the sum by the number of tests taken in all.

Name ______________________ Date __________

Mystery Division

Did you know that you can write a division exercise without using numbers? In the division below, each figure represents a single digit and each type of figure always represents the same digit. Find the division shown below. Use the space provided to show your work.

```
          □△□
    □△ )□△□△
         □△
         ───
          △□△
            □△
          ────
             △
```

What digit does the square represent?

What digit does the triangle represent?

___ ___) ___ ___ ___ ___

1. What strategies did you use to find the digits?

____

____

2. **Analyze** Is more than one answer possible? Explain your thinking.

____

____

Explore It

Use 3 different figures to create a division exercise with only one possible solution. Write your division on a separate sheet of paper and explain how you can ensure that there is only one solution.

Teacher Notes

Explore: Mystery Division

Objective Develop a deeper understanding of division by using models to represent the algorithmic steps of long division.

Using the Explore (Activities to use after Lesson 1)
In this activity, students find the digits represented by different figures in a division exercise. In the example shown, there are two different figures and no remainder. Students should understand that there is only one possible solution in this example. Students should be able to use the guess and check strategy to find the digits represented by the figures. In the Explore It students use a greater number of figures in a division exercise. As the number of figures increases, so does the number of possible solutions.

Math Journal You may wish to have students use their *Math Journals* to answer the Explore It question.

Going Beyond Have students create a division exercise with 4 different figures and only one solution. Students should realize that it is not possible to create a division exercise using 4 figures that has only one solution. However, students can narrow down the possibilities by using the digits 1 and 0 for two of the values and by having no remainder.

Solutions

```
     101
10)1010
    10
    010
     10
      0
```

1. *Answers may vary. Sample:* I used the guess and check strategy.

2. No. There is only one possible answer. Because there is no remainder you know the triangle must be a zero. If you then substitute zeros for all triangles, you see that the second product is zero. Then, if you look at the first and third products, because of the identity property, you know the square must be the digit 1.

Explore It *Answers may vary. Check students' work.* As you increase the number of figures used to represent digits, it becomes harder to ensure that there is only one solution. Using zero as one of the digits and not having a remainder helps narrow the possibilities.

Name ______________________ Date __________

The Division Algorithm

An algorithm is a step-by-step procedure for solving a problem. The word "algorithm" comes from the name of the mathematician, Mohammed ibn-Musa al-Khwarizmi. He lived in Baghdad from about 780 to 850.

You use algorithms when you add, subtract, multiply, and divide.

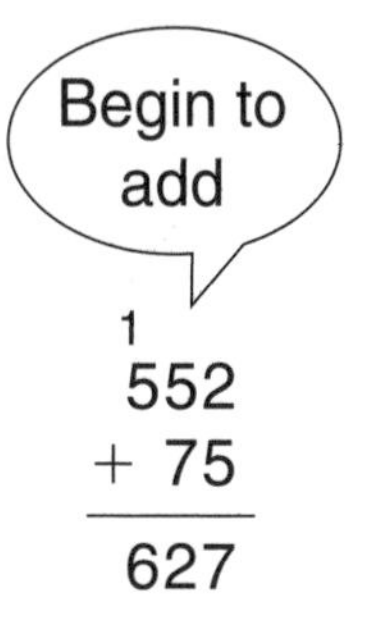

Begin to subtract

$$\begin{array}{r} {\scriptsize 6\ 1} \\ 4\not{7}8 \\ -\ 19 \\ \hline 459 \end{array}$$

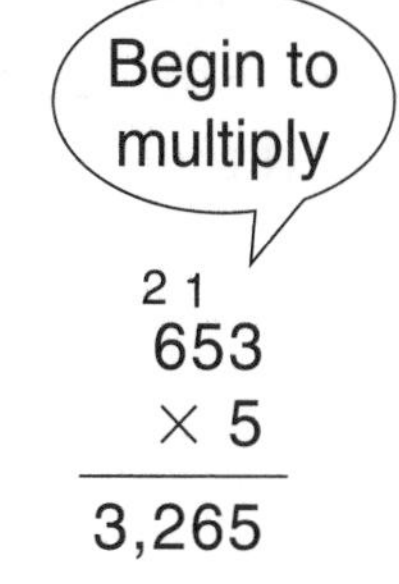

Begin to divide

$$\begin{array}{r} 360\ R5 \\ 12\overline{)4,325} \\ -\ 36 \\ \hline 72 \\ -\ 72 \\ \hline 05 \\ -\ 0 \\ \hline 5 \end{array}$$

1. **Compare** What is similar about the first step in the addition, subtraction, and multiplication algorithms?

____

____

2. **Compare and Contrast** How does the first step in the division algorithm differ from the first step in the other algorithms?

____

____

Extend It

Create an algorithm for division in which the first step is similar to the other algorithms. Compare your algorithm to the traditional algorithm for division. Which is easier to use? Explain why.

Teacher Notes

Extend: The Division Algorithm

Objective Students explore place value as it relates to the division algorithm.

Using the Extend (Activities to use after Lesson 3)

In this activity, students compare the addition, subtraction, and multiplication algorithms. They are asked to look at the first step in each algorithm and contrast this with the first step in the division algorithm. Students are led to an understanding of place value as it relates to each algorithm. Students explore the nature of division itself and how it relates to place value.

Math Journal You may wish to have students use their *Math Journals* to answer the Extend It question.

Going Beyond Have students create algorithms for multiplication, addition, and/or subtraction that start with the greatest place value.

Solutions

1. *Answers may vary. Sample:* In each algorithm, the first step begins with the digit with the least place value.
2. *Answers may vary. Sample:* In the division algorithm, the first step begins with the digit with the greatest place value.

Extend It *Answers may vary. Sample:*

```
    360 R5
   ------
    333
     25
 +   02
   ------
   4325 (12
 -   24
   ------
    301
 -  300
   ------
   399
   4001
 - 3996
   ------
      5
```

The traditional algorithm is easier to use. In the new algorithm you need to estimate larger products. This is more difficult.

Name ______________________ Date __________

Division Choices

Imagine you are a costume designer for a school play and you are making costumes from fabric your school has in stock. The diagram shows the amount of fabric in stock and the amount of fabric needed to make each costume. You need to make 20 shirts, 20 pants, and 10 dresses.

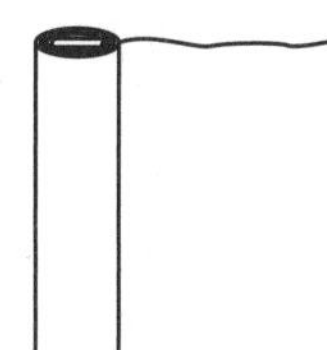

162 feet of plain fabric

2 yards per shirt

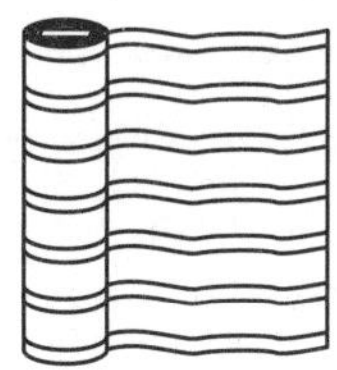

121 feet of striped fabric

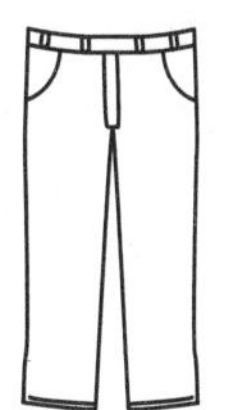

3 yards per pair of pants

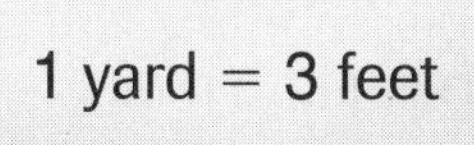

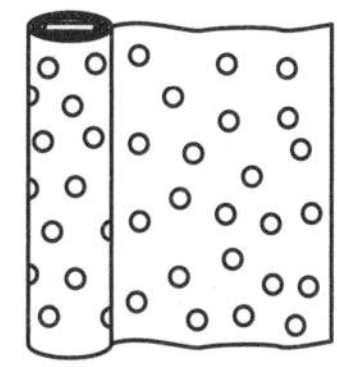

200 feet of polka dot fabric

5 yards per dress

1. **Decide** Make each type of clothing item from the same kind of fabric. For example, use plain fabric for shirts, striped fabric for pants, and polka dot fabric for dresses. You want to have the least amount of each type of fabric left over.

   a. What fabric do you use for the pants? ______________

      shirts? ______________ dresses? ______________

   b. How much of each kind of fabric will you have left over? ______________

   c. Explain how you found your answer. ______________

Connect It

Suppose you can make each type of clothing using different fabrics. You want to make at least 20 shirts, 20 pants, and 10 dresses. Decide what fabrics to use and how many of each type of clothing item to make using that fabric. You want to have the least amount of fabric left over.

Tell how many of each type of clothing you made and the fabric you used. Then tell how much fabric is left.

Teacher Notes

Connect: Division Choices

Objective Students use their long division skills to find solutions with the smallest remainders possible.

Using the Connect (Activities to use after Lesson 5)

In this activity, students consider different ways to use fabric in the most efficient way possible. The remainders in these division problems are equal to the amount of fabric left over. Their goal is to waste the smallest amount of fabric.

Math Journal You may wish to have students use their *Math Journals* to answer the Connect It question.

Going Beyond Tell students that they have to buy the fabric and have them assign prices to each different kind. For example the plain fabric is $1 a yard, the striped is $2 a yard, and the polka dot fabric is $3 a yard. Ask students how their answer will change if they want to spend the least amount possible.

Solutions

1a. 20 polka dot pants, 20 striped shirts, 10 plain dresses.

b. There will be 20 feet of polka dot fabric left over, 12 feet of plain fabric left over, and 1 foot of striped fabric left over.

c. *Answers may vary. Sample:* First, I converted yards to feet for each item. Then, I divided the amound of fabric by the number of feet needed to make each item. This told me how many shirts, pants, and dresses I could make from each type of fabric. I found that the pants can only be made from the polka dot fabric and the dresses can only be made from the plain fabric. That leaves the striped fabric for the shirts.

Connect It *Answers may vary. Sample:* There are many different possible combinations. The best combinations waste the smallest amount of fabric. One answer is to make 8 dresses out of the striped fabric, which leaves 1 foot left over. Then, 24 shirts and 2 pants out of the plain fabric, which leaves none left over. Make 18 pants, 2 dresses, and 1 shirt from the polka dot fabric, which leaves 2 feet left over. The total left over is 3 feet.

Name ______________________ Date __________

Measuring Volume

Imagine you are the head chef at a large restaurant that serves hundreds of people every day. One of your soup recipes calls for exactly 4 gallons of water, but you only have a 3-gallon bucket and a 5-gallon bucket. You need to use the two buckets to measure the correct amount of water.

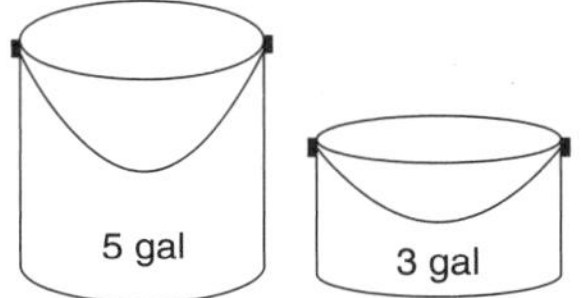

- You can fill the buckets and pour them out as many times as you need to.
- You cannot mark the water level in either bucket.
- You cannot estimate how much water is in each bucket.

1. **Explain** List the steps you take to measure out exactly 4 gallons of water for your recipe.

____

____

2. Is there more than one way to measure the correct amount of water? Explain.

____

Now try another problem. You have a 9-gallon bucket, a 4-gallon bucket, and a 2-gallon bucket.

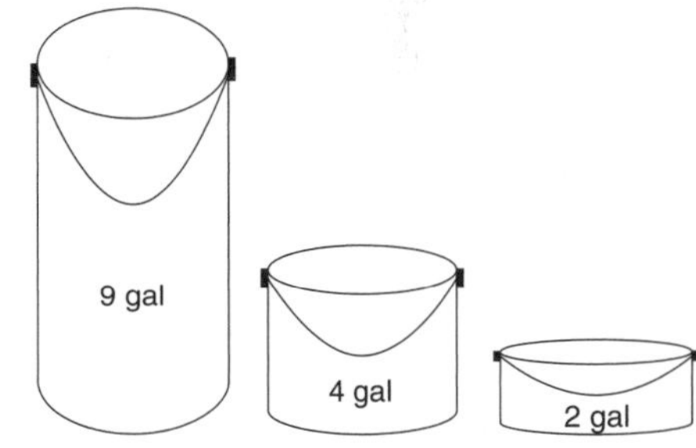

3. List the steps you take in order to have 1 gallon of water in the 4-gallon bucket and 1 gallon of water in the 2-gallon bucket. What steps did you follow?

____

____

____

Explore It

Make up your own word problem using different-sized buckets. Write down the steps you use to solve it.

Teacher Notes

Explore: Measuring Volume

Objective Add and subtract volume measures to solve word problems.

Using the Explore (Activities to use after Lesson 1)

The focus of this chapter is on units of measure and how those measures are used. This activity is intended to enhance students' problem-solving skills. Students solve non-traditional problems with multiple possible solutions. In the Explore It, students should be able to create a similar word problem of their own and describe the steps they took to solve it.

Math Journal You may wish to have students use their *Math Journals* to answer the Explore It question.

Going Beyond Have students discuss why these types of word problems may have multiple solutions.

Solutions

1. *Answers may vary. Sample:*
   1) Fill 3-gallon bucket.
   2) Pour 3-gallon bucket into 5-gallon bucket.
   3) Fill 3-gallon bucket.
   4) Pour 3-gallon bucket into 5-gallon bucket until full, leaving 1 gallon in 3-gallon bucket.
   5) Pour out 5-gallon bucket.
   6) Pour 1 gallon of water from 3-gallon bucket into 5-gallon bucket.
   7) Fill 3-gallon bucket.
   8) Pour 3-gallon bucket into 5-gallon bucket making 4 gallons in the 5-gallon bucket.

2. *Answers may vary. Sample:* Yes. You could also start by filling the 5-gallon bucket first.

3. *Answers may vary. Sample:*
   1) Fill 9-gallon bucket.
   2) Pour 4 gallons from 9-gallon bucket into 4-gallon bucket, leaving 5 gallons in 9-gallon bucket.
   3) Pour out 4-gallon bucket.
   4) Pour 4 gallons from 9-gallon bucket into 4-gallon bucket, leaving 1 gallon in 9-gallon bucket.
   5) Pour 1 gallon from 9-gallon bucket into 2-gallon bucket.
   6) Pour out 4-gallon bucket.
   7) Repeat steps 1–4.
   8) Pour 1 gallon from 9-gallon bucket into 4-gallon bucket.

Explore It *Answers may vary. Check students' work.*

Name ______________________ Date __________

Significant Digits

Scientists need reliable and consistent methods to make measurements. They also need a way to tell other scientists how precise their measurements are. To do this, they use **significant digits**.

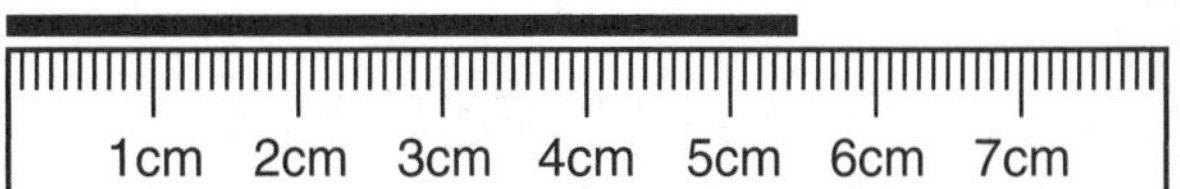

You can use this ruler to measure the length of an object to one tenth of a centimeter. To tell the length of the object to the next decimal place, or hundredth of a centimeter, you can estimate.

For this ruler, the hundredths place is the **first** estimated position so it is the **last** significant digit. The number of significant digits in a scientific measurement tells you how precise the ruler is that made the measurement. The line segment shown above the ruler measures between 5.4 cm and 5.5 cm. You can estimate its length as 5.45 cm.

Write the letter of the ruler that could have been used to make the measurements.

1. 2.2 m ______

a. 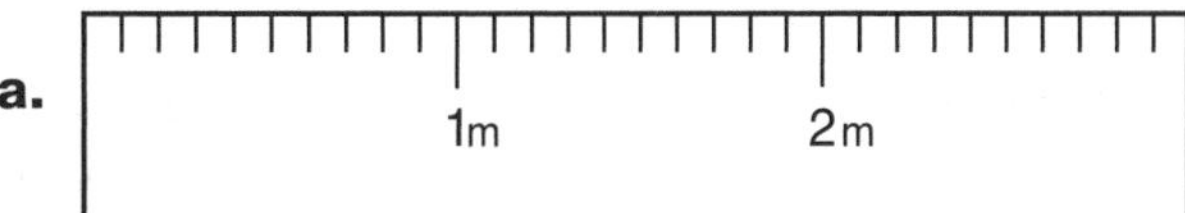

2. 2.7 cm ______

b. 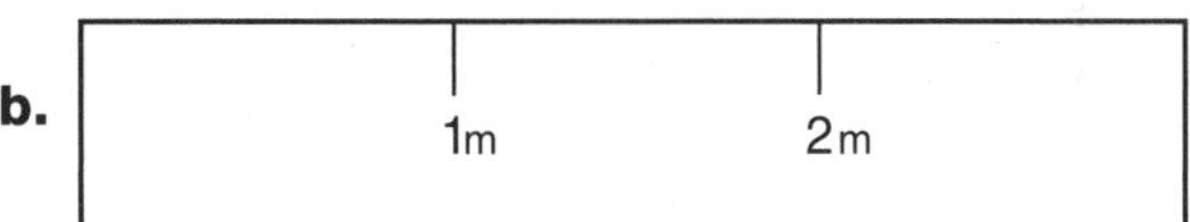

3. 1.82 m ______

c. 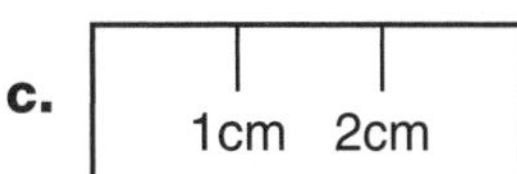

4. **Infer** The length of a line segment is 2.0 cm. Do you think the 0 after the decimal point is a significant digit? Why or why not?

____

Extend It

Why do you think the metric system is used instead of the customary system for scientific measurements?

Teacher Notes

Extend: Significant Digits

Objective Understand how significant digits are used in scientific measurements of length.

Using the Extend (Activities to use after Lesson 4)

All scientific measurements are made using the metric system, primarily because it lends itself to easily reproducible data. In the metric system you can track how accurate each measurement is. Significant digits are used to convey the accuracy of a measurement. This activity is intended as an introduction to how significant digits are used to make measurements. In the Extend It students think critically about why the metric system is used for scientific measurements.

Math Journal You may wish to have students use their *Math Journals* to answer the Extend It question.

Going Beyond Have students find more information about significant digits and how they are used.

Solutions

1. b

2. c

3. a

4. *Answers may vary. Sample:*
Yes. The zero is significant because it means the measurement was made to the nearest millimeter.

Extend It *Answers may vary. Sample:* The metric system is used for scientific measurements because it is based on powers of ten. It is easier to use significant digits in the metric system than in the customary system.

Name ________________________ Date ____________

Conversions

You have already learned how to convert units of measure to other units within the same system. Did you know you can also convert between metric and customary units of measure?

Use the table and a calculator to solve.

Metric and Customary Conversions (≈ means *is approximately equal to*)	
0.4 in. ≈ 1 cm	1 in. = 2.54 cm
3.28 ft ≈ 1 m	1 ft. ≈ 0.3 m
.04 oz ≈ 1 g	1 oz ≈ 28.3 g
2.2 lb ≈ 1 kg	1 lb ≈ 0.45 kg
0.26 gal ≈ 1 L	1 gal ≈ 3.78 L

1. 5 feet ≈ ■ meters
You can multiply to find the answer.

$5 \times 0.3 =$ ______

5 feet ≈ ______ meters

2. Explain How could you use division to find the number of meters in 5 feet?

____

Complete

3. 5 m ≈ ______ ft. **4.** 10 in. = ______ cm **5.** 11 ft. ≈ ______ m

6. 7 kg ≈ ______ lb **7.** 8 L ≈ ______ gal **8.** 24 in. = ______ cm

You can also use the information in the table to estimate a measure in one system when you are given a measure in another system.

Complete

9. 14 gal is about ______ L **10.** 35 lb is about ______ kg

11. 15 cm is about ______ in. **12.** 150 g is about ______ oz

Connect It

How would you find about how many meters there are in 1 yard? How would you find about how many quarts there are in 10 liters? Explain your answers.

Teacher Notes

Connect: Conversions

Objective Calculate and estimate conversions between the metric and customary systems.
Materials calculator

Using the Connect (Activities to use after Lesson 5)

Students have learned to convert units of measure within the metric and customary systems. In this activity, students convert customary units to metric units and metric units to customary units. Students are challenged to explain how to use division instead of multiplication to convert meters to feet. They are also asked to estimate measures in one system given measures in the other system. In the Connect It students have to first apply their knowledge of the customary system before they can calculate the conversion between the two systems.

Math Journal You may wish to have students use their *Math Journals* to answer the Connect It question.

Going Beyond Have students research which countries use the metric system. Have them include a few examples of typical products and their measurements.

Solutions

1. 1.5; 1.5

2. *Answers may vary. Sample:* You could divide 5 by 3.28. There are about 3.28 feet in 1 meter, so divide 5 feet by 3.28 to find about how many meters there are in 5 feet. $5 \div 3.28 = 1.5$. There are about 1.5 meters in 5 feet.

3. 5 meters $\approx$ 16.4 feet

4. 10 in. = 25.4 cm

5. 11 ft $\approx$ 3.3 m

6. 7 kg $\approx$ 15.4 lb

7. 8 L $\approx$ 2.08 gal

8. 24 in. = 60.96 cm

9. *Estimates may vary. Sample:* 56 L

10. *Estimates may vary. Sample:* 18 kg

11. *Estimates may vary. Sample:* 6 in.

12. *Estimates may vary. Sample:* 6 oz

Connect It *Answers may vary. Sample:* You know that 0.3 m $\approx$ 1 foot, and that 3 feet = 1 yard. Multiply to find about how many meters there are in 1 yard: $3 \times 0.3 = 0.9$. There are about 0.9 meters in 1 yard.

You know that 0.26 gal $\approx$ 1 L, and that 4 quarts = 1 gal. Multiply to find about how many quarts there are in 1 liter: $4 \times 0.26 = 1.04$. Multiply by 10 to find about how many quarts there are in 10 liters: $10 \times 1.04 = 10.4$. There are about 10.4 quarts in 10 liters.

Name ________________________ Date __________

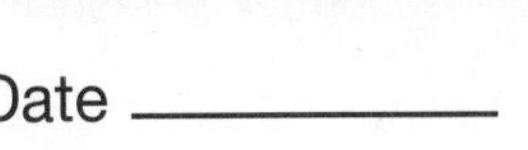

Surveys and Double Bar Graphs

Mrs. Park is a middle school math teacher. Each year she surveys her students. Here are some of her survey results from the past two years.

Year 1

A. Do you plan to join the Math Club next year?

7 boys said yes *8 girls said yes*
7 boys said no *6 girls said no*

B. What is your favorite math topic?

13 students said geometry
10 students said graphing
4 students said algebra
1 student said measurement

Year 2

A. Do you plan to join the Math Club next year?

9 boys said yes *10 girls said yes*
5 boys said no *4 girls said no*

B. What is your favorite math topic?

12 students said geometry
10 students said graphing
3 students said algebra
3 students said measurement

1. On grid paper, create 2 double bar graphs using the data found in the survey results above. Use a different key for each double bar graph. Be sure to give each graph a title.

2. **Infer** Explain why a double bar graph is useful for displaying information found from surveys. ____________________

____

____

____

____

Explore It

On a separate sheet of paper, write another question Mrs. Park could ask her students. Include the results of the question and make a double bar graph using the data.

Teacher Notes

Explore: Surveys and Double Bar Graphs

Objective Use survey results to create double bar graphs.
Materials grid paper

Using the Explore (Activities to use after Lesson 1)

This activity introduces students to surveys and their relationship to double bar graphs. Students must choose how to use the survey results to create their double bar graphs. The critical thinking question emphasizes the importance of graphing data found from surveys. The Explore It allows students to create their own survey question and corresponding double bar graph.

Math Journal You may wish to have students use their *Math Journals* to answer the Explore It question.

Going Beyond Have students create their own survey and survey their classmates. Then have students make double bar graphs using their survey results.

Solutions

1. *Sample:*

Students Who Plan to Join the Math Club

Yes / No

Number of Students: 0 1 2 3 4 5 6 7 8 9 10

Boys in year 1, Girls in year 1, Boys in year 2, Girls in year 2

Students

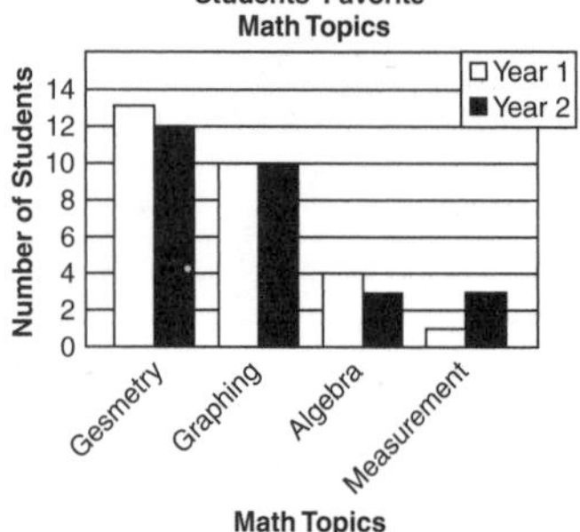

2. *Answers may vary. Sample:* Double bar graphs are helpful when you want to compare data. Data found from surveys is data that can be compared easily.

Explore It *Answers may vary. Sample:* What is your favorite type of class work?

Year 1

7 students said tests
6 students said quizzes
9 students said homework
6 students said classwork

Year 2

4 students said tests
8 students said quizzes
14 students said homework
2 students said classwork

Students' Favorite Type of Class Work

Year 1 / Year 2

Number of Students: 0 2 4 6 8 10 12 14

Tests, Quizzes, Homework, Classwork

Type of Work

Name ______________________ Date __________

Bar Graphs and Line Graphs

Tina is writing a news story about the temperature at different times for two days in Weather City. She uses a double bar graph to present the data.

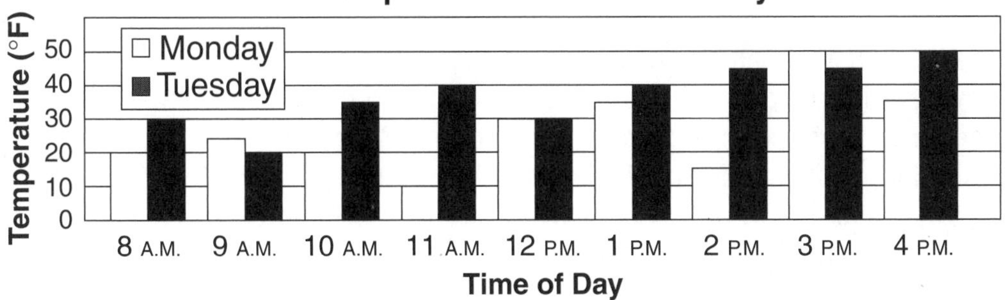

Tina wants to show some of the data using double line graphs.

Complete the double line graphs below.

1.

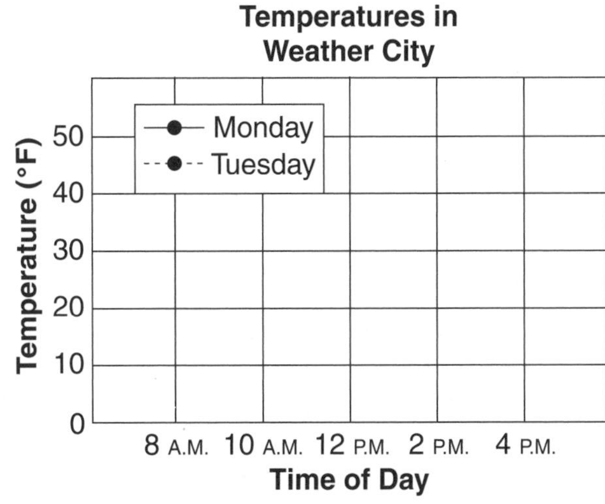

2.

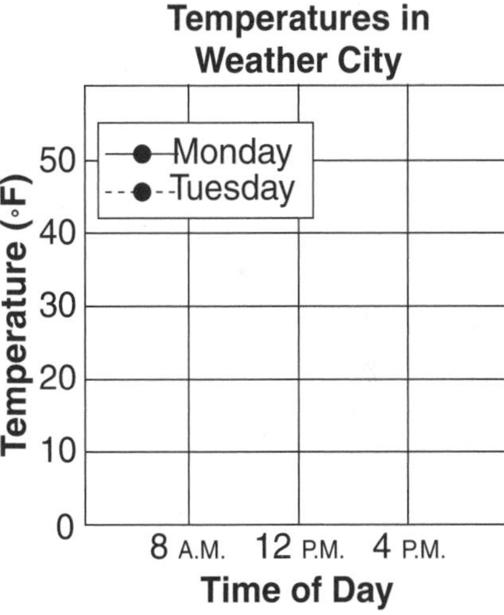

3. **Explain** How do the increments chosen for the horizontal axes affect the way the data is presented? Support your answer with an example. ______________________

____

Extend It

Choose one of the double line graphs above. On a separate sheet of paper, write a short report about the weather using the line graph you chose.

Teacher Notes

Extend: Bar Graphs and Line Graphs

Objective Use a double bar graph to create double line graphs.

Using the Extend (Activities to use after Lesson 3)
In this activity, students convert a double bar graph to double line graphs, then interpret and analyze the data. Students see how changing the labels on the horizontal axes of the double line graphs can affect the presentation of the data. The Extend It asks students to create a news report using one of the double line graphs.

Math Journal You may wish to have students use their *Math Journals* to answer the Extend It.

Going Beyond Have students create an extension of the double bar graph from 5 P.M. to 1 A.M. Then have students create a corresponding double line graph that uses different labels on the horizontal axis.

Solutions

1.

Temperatures in Weather City

Monday
Tuesday
Temperature (°F)
0
10
20
30
40
50
8 A.M.
10 A.M.
12 P.M.
2 P.M.
4 P.M.
Time of Day

2.

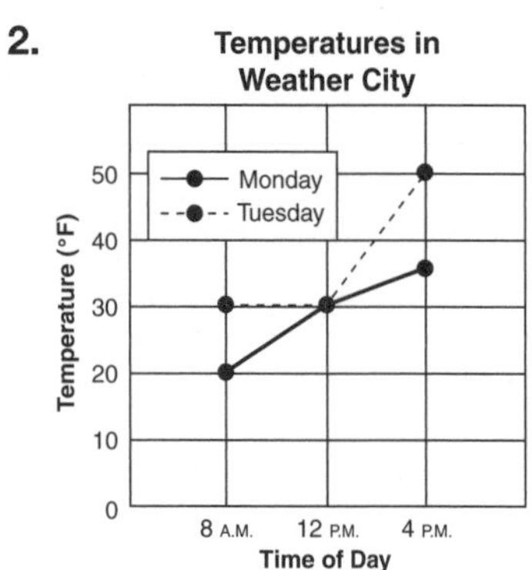

3. *Answers may vary. Sample:* The increments on the horizontal axis of the graph on the right result in fewer of the changes in the data being shown. At 2 P.M. on Monday, the temperature dropped to 15°F, but the graph on the right only shows the temperature increasing during that time.

Extend It *Answers may vary. Sample:* Monday started out very cold. It was only 20°F at 8 A.M. The temperature steadily rose to 35°F at 4 P.M. Temperatures were warmer on Tuesday. It was 30°F at 8 A.M., but rose all the way to 50°F at 4 P.M.

Name ______________________ Date __________

Misleading Histograms

Some histograms can be misleading. When a different interval is chosen to present the data, a histogram can change dramatically. Read the problem below.

Louis and Li collected shells on the beach for 30 days. They recorded how many coral shells they found each day.

25	11	15	3	1	7	8	10	32	7
2	13	4	9	18	21	7	7	16	6
1	22	4	12	5	27	7	9	10	7

Complete each histogram for the data shown above. Use the intervals given.

1.

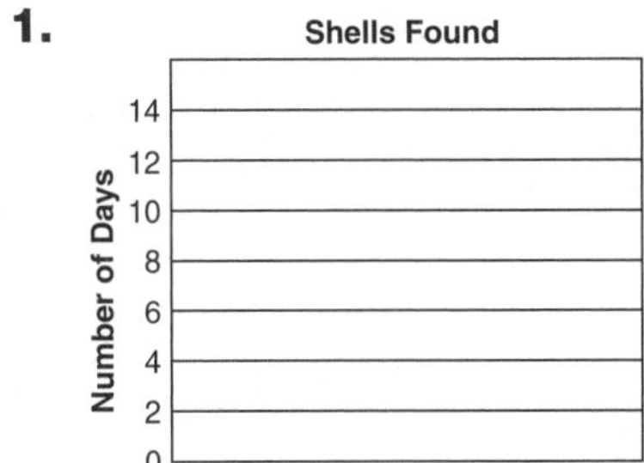

2.

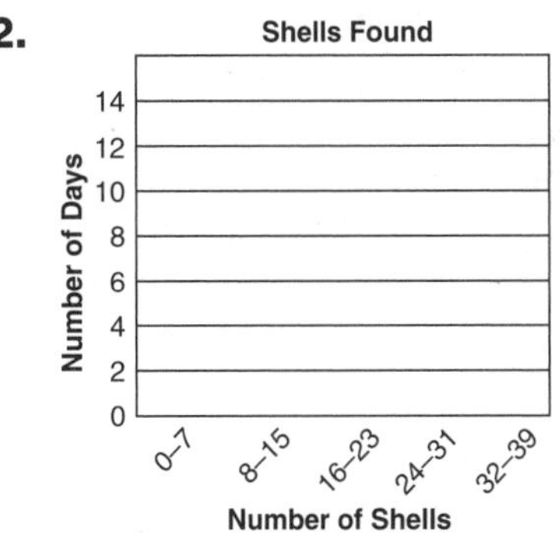

3. Compare and Contrast How are the histograms similar? How are they different?

____

____

____

4. Give an example of how a histogram can be misleading. Use the histograms in Exercises 1 and 2 to support your answer. ____________________

____

____

Connect It

Create two histograms using the data shown above. Choose intervals that are different from the intervals used in Exercises 1 and 2.

Teacher Notes

Connect: Misleading Histograms

Objective Explain how histograms can be misleading when different intervals are used.

Using the Connect (Activities to use after Lesson 5)

Students are introduced to a misleading representation of data by looking at histograms. Students should notice that changing the interval used to present the data can change how the data is interpreted. The Connect It gives students an opportunity to create their own histograms by choosing different intervals.

Math Journal You may wish to have students use their *Math Journals* to answer the Connect It.

Going Beyond Have students make their own set of 2 histograms by creating their own scenario and data. Students should use different intervals in their histograms.

Solutions

1.

Shells Found
Number of Days
14
12
10
8
6
4
2
0
0–6
7–13
14–20
21–27
28–34
Number of Shells

2.

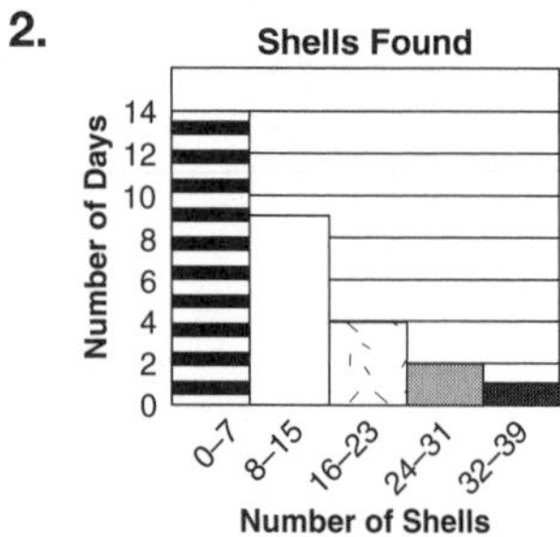

3. *Answers may vary. Sample:* Similar: The intervals with the greater number of shells in both histograms have about the same number of days in them. Different: In the histogram on the left, the second interval has the greatest number of days. In the histogram on the right, the first interval has the greatest number of days.

4. *Answers may vary. Sample:* When one data item is repeated often, that can affect the height of the bar in that interval. The number 7 occurs 6 times in the data. When the 7 is placed in a different interval, it changes the presentation of the data in the histogram.

Connect It *Answers may vary. Sample:*

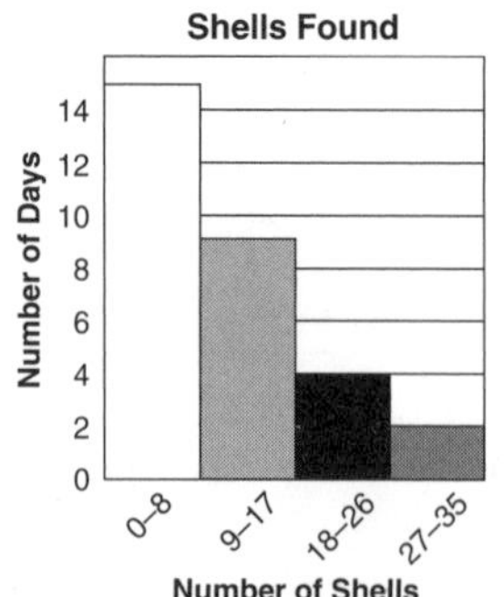

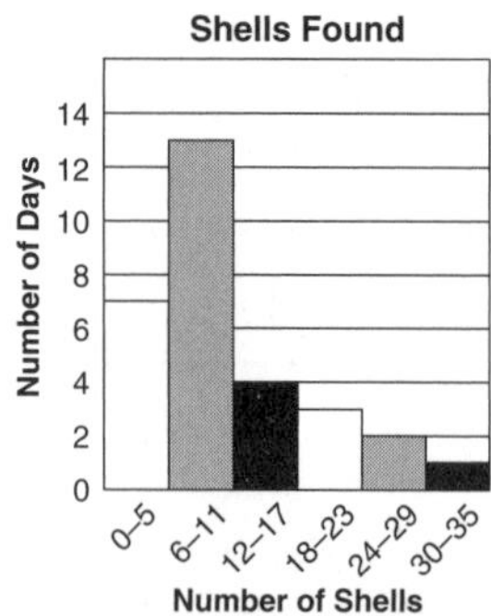

Name ______________________ Date __________

Packaging Preferences

Companies conduct surveys of consumers to determine their preferences for different kinds of packaging.

Suppose the Flagg Cereal Company wants to determine the best way to package its new breakfast cereal. The company surveys 10,000 people and asks them to name their favorite box design.

Here are the results of the poll.

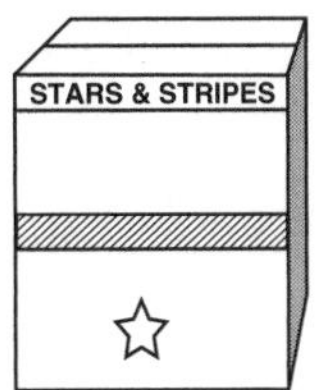

865 votes

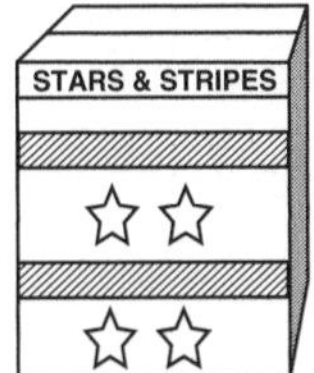

2,565 votes

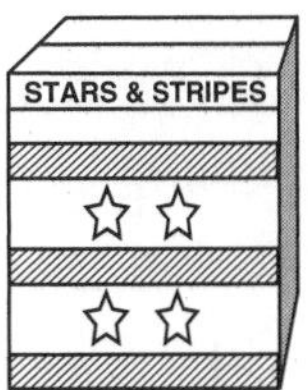

3,024 votes

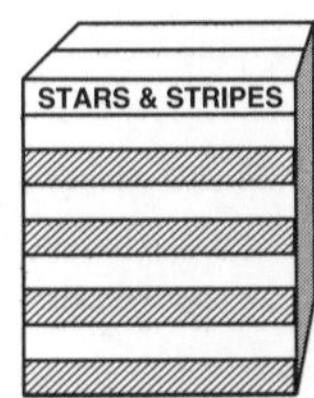

482 votes

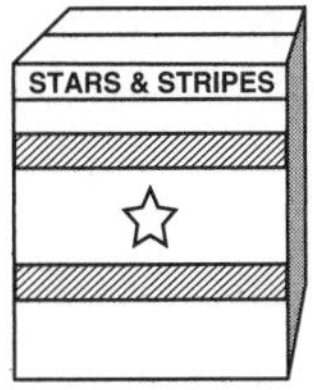

641 votes

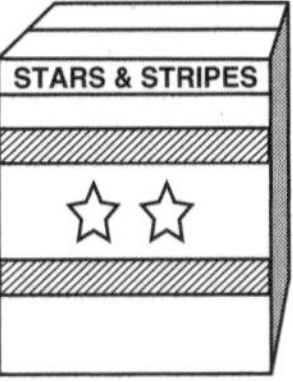

1,042 votes

987 votes

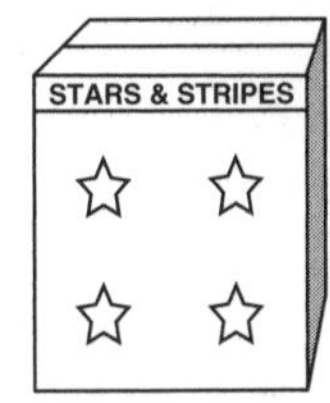

399 votes

1. Which box design received the greatest number of votes?

____

2. Which box design received the fewest votes?

____

3. **Infer** Was there a clear favorite? Was there a clear least favorite? Explain.

____

____

4. **Analyze** Do you see any patterns? What do you think people liked the most about the box design? ______________________________

____

Explore It

Imagine you are the marketing director of the Flagg Cereal Company. Predict which box design will sell best. Can you make a decision based on this data? What additional surveys would you like to conduct? Explain your answers.

Teacher Notes

Explore: Packaging Preferences

Objective Use patterns to predict trends.

Using the Explore (Activities to use after Lesson 1)

In this activity, students look at the results of a fictitious market survey to predict the cereal box design that will sell the most cereal. Each box has a different number of stars and stripes. Students look for a pattern that will help them predict which design will be most profitable.

Math Journal You may wish to have students use their *Math Journals* to answer the Explore It question.

Going Beyond Students could design their own cereal boxes and conduct their own survey of friends and family. In order to determine a trend, they should limit the differences between their designs in order to better identify the elements that people prefer.

Solutions

1. The box design with the greatest number of votes has 3 stripes and 4 stars.
2. The box design with the least number of votes has 4 stars and no stripes.
3. *Answers may vary. Sample:* The top two designs differ by only 459 votes. But the difference between the first and third place design is almost 2,000 votes. There isn't really a clear favorite. The bottom two designs differ by only 83 votes. There definitely isn't a clear least favorite.
4. *Answers may vary. Sample:* The greater the number of stars and stripes, the greater the number of votes received. Since the box is called stars and stripes, it seemed people preferred boxes with many stars and stripes.

Explore It *Answers may vary. Sample:* It seems the best-selling box design has a lot of stars and stripes. However, since the results for the top two designs were very close, I would want to do some additional research. If I were the marketing director, I would want to conduct another survey using just the top two designs.

Name ______________________________ Date ____________

Measures of Greatness

What makes a great baseball player? There are hundreds of different statistics collected about professional baseball players. These include the number of games played, the number of times at bat, the number of runs scored, and the number of home runs hit.

The stem and leaf plot below represents the number of home runs scored each year for two of baseball's greatest players, Babe Ruth and Hank Aaron.

Boston Red Sox
New York Yankees
1914–1935

Babe Ruth's Home Runs	
Stem	Leaf
0	0 2 3 4 6
1	1
2	2 5 9
3	4 5
4	1 1 6 6 6 7 9
5	4 4 9
6	0

Milwaukee Braves
Atlanta Braves
Milwaukee Brewers
1954–1976

Hank Aaron's Home Runs	
Stem	Leaf
1	0 2 3
2	0 4 6 7 9
3	0 2 4 4 8 9 9
4	0 0 4 4 4 4 5 7

1. Find the mean, median, mode, and range for each player. Use a calculator if necessary.

____

____

2. Which player has the higher mean? ____________

3. Which player has the higher median? ____________

4. Which player has the higher mode? ____________

5. Which player has the wider range? ____________

Extend It

Who is the better player? Can you tell from this data? Which statistic will you use to make your decision? Why? What additional information would help you to decide?

Teacher Notes

Extend: Measures of Greatness

Objective Use data in a stem and leaf plot to calculate the mean, median, mode, and range.
Materials calculator

Using the Extend (Activities to use after Lesson 3)

Students are given data for home runs hit by Babe Ruth and Hank Aaron in the form of a stem and leaf plot. They calculate the mean, median, mode, and range for each player. The Extend It asks students to decide who they think is the better player based on this information. They are guided to think about each measure of central tendency and what it represents.

Math Journal You may wish to have students use their *Math Journals* to answer the Extend It questions.

Going Beyond Have students look at additional statistics for Ruth and Aaron, such as runs batted in or number of times at bat, to help them decide who is the better player. Adding additional statistics provides more data upon which to base a decision. However, students will have to define what they feel are the most important qualities in a great baseball player.

Solutions

1. Babe Ruth:
   Mean 32.4
   Median 38
   Mode 46
   Range 0–60

   Hank Aaron:
   Mean 32.8
   Median 34
   Mode 44
   Range 10–47
2. Hank Aaron has the higher mean.
3. Babe Ruth has the higher median.
4. Babe Ruth has the higher mode.
5. Babe Ruth has the wider range.

Extend It *Answers may vary. Sample:* Hank Aaron and Babe Ruth are comparable players, so this is a difficult question to answer. Aaron's mean is higher, but Ruth is better than Aaron in the rest of the statistics. Babe Ruth had a wider range than Aaron. Aaron was much more consistent. For this reason, Aaron might be considered the better player. It is a very close call. Additional statistics, such as runs batted in, could help.

Name ________________________ Date ____________

Agenian Ages

The fictional planet Agenia has 9 different countries. A census was taken to determine the average age of the population in each country. This chart shows the results.

Age Statistics of People in Countries of Planet Agenia									
	Ionia	**Triandia**	**Quadonia**	**Pentonia**	**Hexonia**	**Septenia**	**Octognia**	**Novembia**	**Centenia**
Mean	65	75	52	47	65	59	50	21	55
Median	72	56	47	33	75	70	52	29	42
Mode	60	45	25	19	55	85	48	35	57
Range	1–92	1–100	1–88	1–65	1–99	1–99	1–98	1–50	1–72

Use the data in the chart to answer the questions.

1. Which country has the highest mean age? lowest mean age?

   ____

2. Which country has the highest median age? lowest median age?

   ____

3. Which country has the highest mode? lowest mode?

   ____

4. Which country has the widest range? narrowest range?

   ____

5. **Explain** Which measure would you use to best describe the age of the population for each country? ____________________ Why? ____________________

6. **Infer** How could it be possible for a country to have both the highest and lowest of any two of these statistics? ____________________

Connect It

What could be causing the differences between the statistics in a single country? For example, why would a country have a very low mode, while also having a high median?

Teacher Notes

Connect: Agenian Ages

Objective Use the differences between mean, median, mode, and range, to draw conclusions.
Materials calculator

Using the Connect (Activities to use after Lesson 5)

In this activity, students are given data regarding the average age of the population for 9 countries on a fictional planet called Agenia. They are asked to find the country with the oldest and youngest people, and to decide which measure of central tendency best represents their answer.

Math Journal You may wish to have students use their *Math Journals* to answer the Connect It question.

Going Beyond Have students write a newspaper article comparing two of the countries and explaining the differences in the average age.

Solutions

1. Highest mean: Triandia, 75
   Lowest mean: Novembia, 21
2. Highest median: Hexonia, 75
   Lowest median: Novembia, 29
3. Highest mode: Septenia, 85
   Lowest mode: Pentonia, 19
4. Widest range: Triandia, 1–100
   Narrowest range: Novembia, 1–50
5. *Answers may vary. Sample:* The median is often considered the best measure to describe the age of the population for each country, as it is the middle number. So, half the population will be above that number and half below. The mean can be skewed by outliers. The mode could be just 2 people.
6. *Answers may vary. Sample:* A country could have a low median, but a high mode if there are a lot of people who are one particular age, with many people at much lower ages.

Connect It *Answers may vary. Sample:* The differences between the statistics in a single country could be due to having many young children, or a large number of very old people in a country with many young people.

Name ______________________ Date ____________

Identify Prime and Composite Numbers

Divisibility rules can help you identify prime and composite numbers. For example, every even number is divisible by 2. Therefore, all even numbers other than 2 are composite.

For Exercises 1–4, identify each number as prime or composite. For each composite number, write the divisibility rule(s) you used.

1. 32 ______________________

2. 25 ______________________

3. 29 ______________________

4. 80 ______________________

5. The number 51 is a composite number. What divisibility rule can you use to identify 51 as a composite number?

____

6. The number 91 is a composite number. Is there a divisibility rule you can use to identify 91 as a composite number? Explain how you know.

____

7. **Analyze** Would you have predicted that 51 and 91 were composite numbers? Why do you think these two numbers might be mistakenly identified as prime?

____

Explore It

List other composite numbers that might be mistakenly identified as prime. On a separate sheet of paper, describe what these numbers have in common and explain why they might be mistakenly identified as prime.

Teacher Notes

Explore: Identify Prime and Composite Numbers

Objective Use divisibility rules to identify prime and composite numbers.

Using the Explore (Activities to use after Lesson 1)

Divisibility rules learned in Chapter 4 can be very helpful in identifying prime and composite numbers. Students discover that composite numbers that are multiples of prime numbers may be erroneously identified as prime numbers. The Explore It asks students to write a rule that describes these composite numbers.

Math Journal You may wish to have students use their *Math Journals* for the Explore It.

Going Beyond Have students list prime numbers that might be identified as composite numbers and consider what these numbers have in common.

Solutions

1. Composite. *Answers may vary. Sample:* the divisibility rule for 2.
2. Composite; the divisibility rule for 5.
3. Prime
4. Composite. *Answers may vary. Sample:* The divisibility rule for 10.
5. The divisibility rule for 3.
6. No. There is no divisibility rule you can use for 91. *Answers may vary. Sample:* I checked the divisibility rules for 2, 3, 4, 5, 6, 9, and 10. None of the rules help identify 91 as a composite number.
7. *Answers may vary. Sample:* I would not have predicted they were composite numbers. I think these numbers are often identified as prime because they are numbers ending with 1 and many numbers ending with 1 are prime.

Explore It *Answers may vary. Sample:* 221 and 161. They are both multiples of two prime numbers and they both end with the number 1. They might be mistakenly identified as prime because they end with the number 1.

Name ______________________ Date __________

Investigating Fractions

The square at the right represents one whole.

For each given section of the square, write the fraction of the whole that it represents.

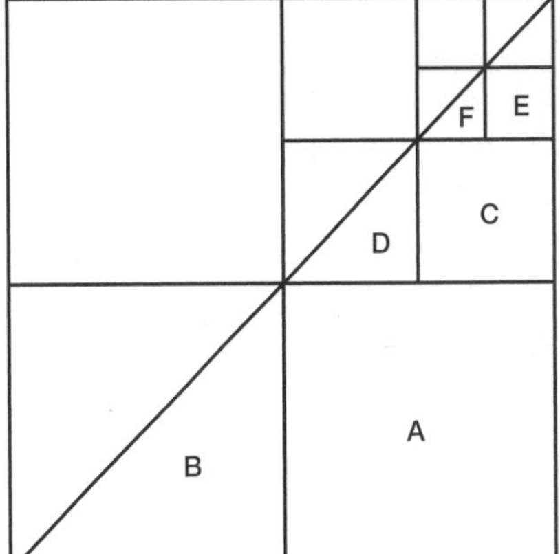

1. Square A ______________
2. Triangle B ______________
3. Square C ______________
4. Triangle D ______________
5. Square E ______________
6. Triangle F ______________

7. **Analyze** If you continue dividing the square this way, will you create a figure that represents $\frac{1}{512}$ of the square? Why or why not?

____

____

8. **Explain** Do you think there is a limit to the number of times that a square can be divided into equal parts? Why or why not?

____

____

Extend It

How can you divide a square into figures representing equal thirds and equal ninths? On a separate sheet of paper, draw a square. Use straight lines to divide the square into sections representing the fractions $\frac{1}{3}$, $\frac{1}{9}$, and $\frac{1}{81}$. Label the sections representing each fraction.

Teacher Notes

Extend: Investigating Fractions

Objective Investigate equivalent fractions by dividing squares along their lines of symmetry.

Using the Extend (Activities to use after Lesson 5)
Squares can be divided and subdivided along their lines of symmetry into equivalent sections that steadily diminish by a power of 2. In this activity, students investigate fractions represented by figures that were created by dividing and subdividing squares along lines of symmetry. The Extend It encourages students to consider methods for dividing a square to represent fractions that diminish by a power of 3.

Math Journal You may wish to have students use their *Math Journals* for the Extend It.

Going Beyond Have students experiment with dividing and subdividing other figures along their lines of symmetry and other lines. Have them describe their results in fractional terms.

Solutions

1. $\frac{1}{4}$
2. $\frac{1}{8}$
3. $\frac{1}{16}$
4. $\frac{1}{32}$
5. $\frac{1}{64}$
6. $\frac{1}{128}$
7. Yes. *Answers may vary. Sample:* Each fraction that represents a section of the square decreases by a power of 2. Square A is $\frac{1}{2^2}$, triangle B is $\frac{1}{2^3}$, square C is $\frac{1}{2^4}$. Since 512 is a power of 2, you can create a figure that represents $\frac{1}{512}$ of the square.
8. No. *Answers may vary. Sample:* You can keep forming new squares that can be divided into even smaller squares, although eventually they will be too small to draw.

Extend It *Answers may vary. Sample:*

$\frac{1}{81}$

$\frac{1}{3}$

$\frac{1}{9}$

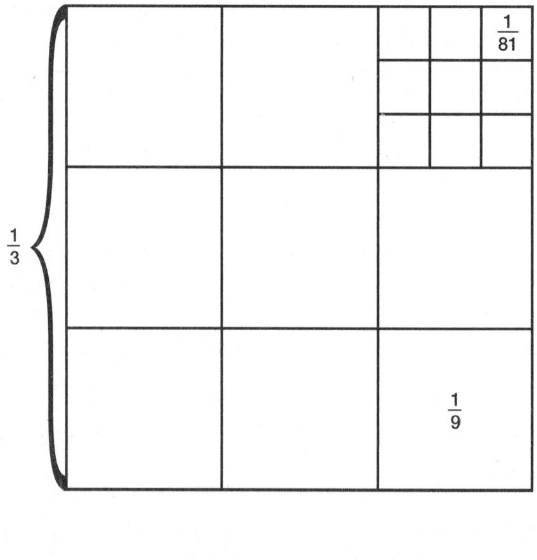

Name ________________________ Date __________

The Stock Market

Businesses sell shares in their companies in order to raise money. The prices of these shares are listed on the stock market. Today, stocks have decimal prices. For hundreds of years, though, stock prices were listed as mixed numbers.

The table shows the price per share of stock for 6 companies. The stock prices are shown as mixed numbers in Year 1 and as decimals in Year 2.

Price Per Share of Stock (in dollars)		
	Year 1	**Year 2**
Transworld Cinema	$12\frac{3}{4}$	13.95
Skyway Airlines	$17\frac{3}{4}$	12.10
Blue Earth Foods	$8\frac{1}{4}$	10.40
New Thing Clothing	$14\frac{1}{2}$	13.50
Galactic Computers	$18\frac{3}{4}$	14.25
Acme Motors	$17\frac{1}{4}$	20.75

1. Which stock had the greatest change in price from Year 1 to Year 2? ____________

By how much did the price increase or decrease? ____________

2. What was the price in dollars and cents of 10 shares of Transworld Cinema stock in Year 1? ____________

What was the price of 10 shares in Year 2? ____________

3. **Analyze** Suppose you purchased 3 shares of one company's stock and 2 shares of another company's stock in Year 1. You spent $59.25. What two companies' stocks did you purchase?

____

Connect It

Why do you think the stock market changed their listings from mixed numbers to decimals? On a separate sheet of paper, explain your answer.

Teacher Notes

Connect: The Stock Market

Objective Use the mixed number format of stock market prices to relate mixed numbers and decimals.

Using the Connect (Activities to use after Lesson 9)

For most of the more than 200-year history of the New York Stock Exchange, stock prices were listed as mixed numbers. Since these stock prices represent monetary values, they offer an opportunity to apply the skill of converting between mixed numbers and decimals. In this exercise, students use a fictitious stock market chart to assess and compare the mixed-number values of stocks with decimal values of stock. The Connect It encourages students to consider why the stock market changed their listings from mixed numbers to decimals.

Math Journal You may wish to have students use their *Math Journals* for the Connect It.

Going Beyond Have students look at stock listings in a newspaper. Ask them to identify stock values in dollars and cents. Have students investigate the meanings of stock highs, lows, and changes.

Solutions

1. Skyway Airlines; the price decreased by $5.65.
2. $127.50, $139.50
3. 3 shares of Blue Earth Foods and 2 shares of Acme Motors

Connect It *Answers may vary. Sample:* I think the stock market changed their listings from mixed numbers to decimals because our monetary system is based on decimals. If the stock prices are listed as decimals, it is easy to see the price per share as dollars and cents.

Name ______________________ Date ____________

Estimation Decisions

When you estimate fraction sums and differences you can make an estimate that is more or less than the exact answer. The decision you make should be based on the situation. Look at the situations shown below.

Situation 1: You cannot bring more than 25 lbs in your carry-on bag on an airplane. You have the following items to pack:

Item	Weight
Laptop	$9\frac{1}{4}$ lb
Book	$2\frac{3}{4}$ lb
Toiletries	$12\frac{1}{2}$ lb
Bag of snacks	$1\frac{1}{8}$ lb

Situation 2: There is no charge for shipping if you order 10 or more pounds of dog treats from an online pet food store. You want to order the following:

Item	Weight of Package
Dog biscuits	$2\frac{1}{2}$ lb
Rawhide treats	$3\frac{1}{4}$ lb
Bone chews	$4\frac{1}{8}$ lb

Use the situations above to answer Questions 1 and 2. Decide whether to overestimate or underestimate. Explain your decisions.

1. Can you take all of the items in Situation 1 in your carry-on bag? ____________

____

2. Will there be a charge for shipping in Situation 2? ____________

____

3. Create Describe a situation in which you would overestimate a sum involving fractions. Describe a situation in which you would underestimate a sum. Write a question for each situation. ____________

____

Explore It

Is it possible to overestimate the difference when fractions are involved? Is it possible to underestimate the difference? Explain using examples.

Teacher Notes

Explore: Estimation Decisions

Objective Decide when to overestimate or underestimate a sum involving fractions.

Using the Explore (Activities to use after Lesson 1)

This activity provides the opportunity for students to make logical decisions about when to overestimate or underestimate a fractional sum. Students learn that they can round up or use front-end estimation depending on the problem-solving situation. The Explore It encourages students to apply what they learned about over- and under-estimation of fractional sums to fractional differences and then support their conclusions with examples.

Math Journal You may wish to have students use their *Math Journals* to answer the Explore It question.

Going Beyond Have students support or reject the following hypothesis: It is impossible to use front-end estimation to overestimate a fractional sum. Students should realize this is true because in front-end estimation the fractional parts of the sums are dropped and therefore the estimate is always less than the exact sum.

Solutions

1. *Answers may vary. Sample:* No. You cannot take all the items. I would overestimate to be sure I do not go over the allowed weight.
2. *Answers may vary. Sample:* Yes. There will be a charge for shipping. I would underestimate to be sure to qualify for free shipping.
3. *Answers may vary. Sample:* Overestimate: You can travel up to 200 miles on a tank of gas. Do you have enough gas to travel $120\frac{3}{4}$ miles in one day and $179\frac{3}{4}$ miles the next day without refueling? Underestimate: A report needs to be 5 or more pages in length. Yesterday you wrote $2\frac{1}{4}$ pages and today you wrote $2\frac{1}{2}$ pages. Is the report finished?

Explore It *Answers may vary. Sample:* Yes. Using front-end estimation for the number you are subtracting can overestimate the difference. For example, to overestimate the difference of $5\frac{1}{2} - 3\frac{3}{4}$ estimate $5 - 3 = 2$. Two is greater than the exact difference, $1\frac{3}{4}$. You can round up to underestimate this same difference: $5\frac{1}{2} - 3\frac{3}{4}$ rounds up to $5\frac{1}{2} - 4 = 1\frac{1}{2}$. One and one-half is less than the exact difference, $1\frac{3}{4}$.

Name ______________________________ Date ____________

Fraction Number Patterns

One way to describe a number pattern is to look at two consecutive numbers in the sequence and use that information to guess the rule used to form the pattern. You can check your rule with other numbers in the series.

Find the rule for the pattern in this number series:

$\frac{1}{8}, \frac{1}{4}, \frac{3}{8}, \frac{1}{2}, \frac{5}{8}, \frac{3}{4}, \frac{7}{8}, 1$

Guess: How can you go from $\frac{1}{8}$ to $\frac{1}{4}$? Add $\frac{1}{8}$.

Check: Apply your rule to the first number in the series:

$\frac{1}{8} + \frac{1}{8} = \frac{2}{8} = \frac{1}{4}$.

Check to see if your rule works for other numbers in the series:

$\frac{1}{4} + \frac{1}{8} =$ ______ $\frac{3}{8} + \frac{1}{8} =$ ______

The rule for the pattern for this series is ______________________________.

Find the rule for each number series.

1. $\frac{1}{10}, \frac{1}{2}, \frac{9}{10}, 1\frac{3}{10}, 1\frac{7}{10}$

Guess: ______ Check: ______________

Rule: ______________________

2. $\frac{5}{16}, \frac{5}{8}, \frac{15}{16}, 1\frac{1}{4}, 1\frac{9}{16}, 1\frac{7}{8}$

Guess: ______ Check: ______________

Rule: ______________________

3. Hypothesize Describe the pattern of addition that is used to create this number series: $0, \frac{1}{8}, \frac{3}{8}, \frac{3}{4}, 1\frac{1}{4}, 1\frac{7}{8}$. Use the pattern to tell the next number in the series.

____

4. Compare and Contrast Compare the patterns for the number series in Exercises 2 and 3.

____

Extend It

On a separate sheet of paper, create a number series with 5 or more numbers that follows a pattern using addition of fractions.

Teacher Notes

Extend: Fraction Number Patterns

Objective Use fraction addition to identify number patterns and missing numbers in a series.

Using the Extend (Activities to use after Lesson 3)
In this activity, students use a guess and check strategy to identify patterns in a fraction number series. Students then extend the skill to finding missing numbers in a number series by identifying and then applying the rule for the pattern. In the Extend It students use what they learned to create their own fraction number series using a rule for a pattern that they make up on their own.

Math Journal You may wish to have students use their *Math Journals* to answer the Extend It question.

Going Beyond Have students make up a word problem in which they must identify a fraction number pattern in order to solve the problem.

Solutions

$\frac{1}{4} + \frac{1}{8} = \frac{3}{8}$

$\frac{3}{8} + \frac{1}{8} = \frac{1}{2}$

The rule for the pattern for this series is add $\frac{1}{8}$.

1. Guess: Add $\frac{4}{10}$

Check: $\frac{1}{10} + \frac{4}{10} = \frac{5}{10} = \frac{1}{2}$

$\frac{1}{2} + \frac{4}{10} = \frac{9}{10}$

Rule: Add $\frac{4}{10}$ or Add $\frac{2}{5}$

2. Guess: Add $\frac{5}{16}$

Check: $\frac{5}{16} + \frac{5}{16} = \frac{10}{16} = \frac{5}{8}$

$\frac{5}{8} + \frac{5}{16} = \frac{15}{16}$

Rule: Add $\frac{5}{16}$

3. Start by adding $\frac{1}{8}$, then increase the amount you add by $\frac{1}{8}$ each time. Add $\frac{1}{8}$, then $\frac{2}{8}$, then $\frac{3}{8}$, then $\frac{4}{8}$, then $\frac{5}{8}$. The next number in the series is $2\frac{5}{8}$.

4. *Answers may vary. Sample:* Alike: both patterns follow an addition rule to create the number series. Different: in Exercise 2 the rule is to add the same amount to each number in the series. In Exercise 3 the rule is to add an increasing amount to each number.

Extend It *Answers may vary. Sample:* $\frac{1}{3}$, $\frac{5}{6}$, $1\frac{1}{3}$, $1\frac{5}{6}$, $2\frac{1}{3}$.

Name ______________________________ Date ______________

Math and Weather

Precipitation can be in the form of hail, sleet, rain, mist, or snow.

The data to the right shows the average precipitation for weather stations in U.S. cities for the summer months of June through August.

Precipitation in inches			
City	**June**	**July**	**August**
Albany, NY	$3\frac{7}{10}$	$3\frac{1}{2}$	$3\frac{7}{10}$
Houston, TX	$5\frac{2}{5}$	$3\frac{1}{5}$	$3\frac{4}{5}$
Tampa, FL	$5\frac{1}{2}$	$6\frac{1}{2}$	$7\frac{3}{5}$
Barrow, AK	$\frac{3}{10}$	$\frac{9}{10}$	1
Denver, CO	$1\frac{3}{5}$	$2\frac{1}{5}$	$1\frac{4}{5}$

1. One city listed in the chart has a combined precipitation of 7 inches for two months and a difference of $\frac{3}{5}$ inches for the same two months.

   Which city is this? Which two months? ______________________

2. **Analyze** The normal precipitation for September in one of the listed cities is $\frac{2}{5}$ inch less than its August precipitation. In September this city's precipitation is normally $3\frac{3}{10}$ inches. Which city is this? ______________

3. **Compare** How many more inches of precipitation does Tampa, Florida get during June, July, and August than Denver, Colorado? ______________

4. **Create** Write 3 questions about the data in the table using addition and 3 questions using subtraction. Answer your questions.

   ____

   ____

   ____

Connect It

Based on the data shown in the table, what conclusion can you make about the relationship between location and precipitation? Use a map of the United States to help you with your conclusion. Explain on a separate sheet of paper.

Teacher Notes

Connect: Math and Weather

Objective Solve multi-step fraction problems using weather data.

Using the Connect (Activities to use after Lesson 6)

In this activity, students use data about typical precipitation amounts in selected cities to solve multi-step word problems. The problems require students to use what they have learned about adding and subtracting fractions and mixed numbers to interpret and compare the given data. The Connect it challenges students to synthesize the information in the data in order to draw a sensible conclusion about the relationship between precipitation and geographical location.

Math Journal You may wish to have students use their *Math Journals* to answer the Connect It question.

Going Beyond Have students research the monthly precipitation for the weather station nearest their own city. Have them use the data to predict the amount of precipitation they can expect over the next 3 months.

Solutions

1. Houston; July and August
2. Albany
3. 14 more inches
4. *Answers may vary. Sample:* Addition: What is the total precipitation for Denver for June and July? for Houston? for Albany? $3\frac{4}{5}$ inches; $8\frac{3}{5}$ inches; $7\frac{1}{5}$ inches. Subtraction: How many more inches of precipitation does Tampa get in July than Barrow? How many more inches does Tampa get in August than in June? How many more inches does Albany get in August than Denver? $5\frac{3}{5}$ more inches; $2\frac{1}{10}$ more inches; $1\frac{9}{10}$ more inches.

Connect It *Answers may vary. Sample:* Generally, the further north a city is, the less precipitation it gets. Conversely, the further south a city is, the more precipitation it gets.

Name ______________________ Date ____________

Add and Subtract Decimals

You have used a number line to add and subtract whole numbers. You can also use a number line to add and subtract decimals. Look at the examples below.

Example A: Add. $3.4 + 0.7 = n$

Example B: Subtract. $5.0 - 1.4 = n$

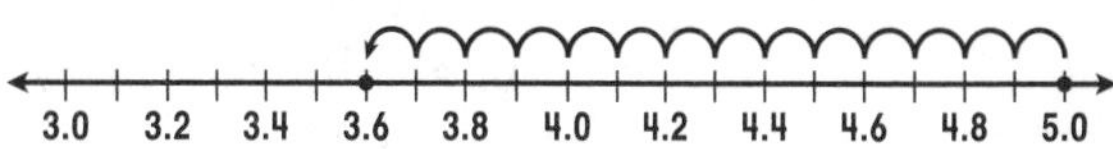

1. **Explain** In each example, how do you know where to begin on the number line? How do you know where to end?

   ____

2. **Interpret** What does the interval between each tick mark represent? How do you know?

   ____

   ____

3. What is the sum shown on the number line in Example A? What is the difference shown on the number line in Example B?

   ____

4. How would you modify the number line in Example A to find $4.8 + 0.5$? How would you modify the number line in Example B to find $3.2 - 1.5$?

   ____

   ____

5. **Infer** Would a number line be a useful tool to use to find the sum of 23.14 and 12.67? Why or why not?

   ____

Explore It

On a separate sheet of paper, draw a number line to find the sum of 1.15 and 0.20. Then use your number line to find $1.25 - 0.05$.

Teacher Notes

Explore: Add and Subtract Decimals

Objective Use a number line to add and subtract decimals.

Using the Explore (Activities to use after Lesson 1)
In this activity, students analyze how a number line can be used to add and subtract decimals. Students explain and interpret two sample number lines that show addition and subtraction. Students also use critical thinking skills to infer when a number line is a sensible tool to use and when it is not. In the Explore It, students apply what they know about number lines to create their own number line to add and subtract hundredths decimals.

Math Journal You may wish to have students use their *Math Journals* to answer the Explore It question.

Going Beyond Have students compare how creating a number line is similar to creating a bar graph. Students should realize that both require a scale of numbers with the same increment between each number in the scale.

Solutions

1. *Answers may vary. Sample:* In Example A, you begin at the tick mark that represents the first number, 3.4. You end by counting 7 tenths to the right because when you add on a number line you move to the right. In Example B, you begin at the tick mark that represents the first number, 5.0 and move 1 and 4 tenths to the left because you move left when you subtract.
2. The interval between each tick mark represents 1 tenth. *Answers may vary. Sample:* You know because every other tick mark is labeled and they increase in increments of 2 tenths.
3. Sum: 4.1; difference: 3.6
4. *Answers may vary. Sample:* In Example A, extend the number line to the right so that you could move 5 tenths to the right of 4.8. In Example B, extend the number line to the left so that you could move 1 and 5 tenths to the left of 3.2.
5. *Answers may vary. Sample:* No, because you need to move too far to the right on a number line to show exactly 12.67 more than 23.14. The number line would be too long to draw conveniently.

Explore It *Answers may vary. Check students' number lines. Sample:*

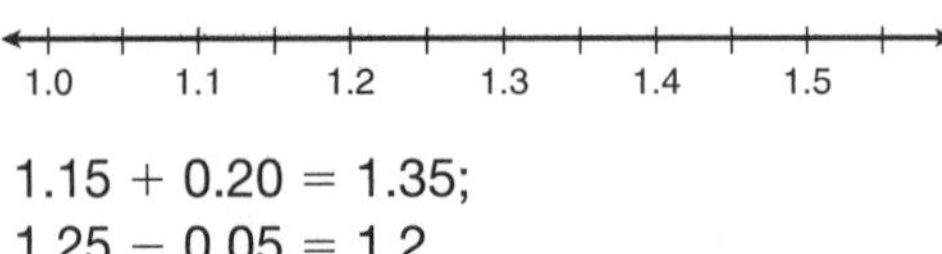

1.15 + 0.20 = 1.35;
1.25 − 0.05 = 1.2

Name ______________________________ Date ____________

Identify and Correct Errors

Students sometimes make errors when solving problems with decimals. Some errors involve the operation used to solve the problem, while other errors are computational. Each example below has one specific error.

Example A **Problem:** Seth drove 123.2 miles on Monday and 23.45 miles on Tuesday. How many miles did he drive in all? **Solution:** 1 2 3.2 + 2 3.4 5 3 5 7.7	**Example B** **Problem:** Juan has a piece of ribbon 38 cm long. He cuts off a piece that is 5.76 cm. How much ribbon is left? **Solution:** 38 − 5.76 33.76
Example C **Problem:** Last week Aaron ran 7.4 miles. This week he ran 0.8 miles more than last week. How many miles did Aaron run this week? **Solution:** 7.4 − 0.8 6.2	

1. **Classify** For each example above, classify the error as a computational error or an operation error. Explain your answers.

____

2. **Analyze** What error was made in Example A? Find the correct solution.

____

3. Explain how to solve the problem in Example B correctly.

____

4. **Decide** How could you decide which operation to use to solve the problem in Example C? Use your decision to correct the error in the solution.

____

Extend It

On a separate sheet of paper, make a checklist for adding and subtracting decimals based on the errors you identified.

Teacher Notes

Extend: Identify and Correct Errors

Objective Identify and correct errors in problems that involve adding and subtracting decimals.

Using the Extend (Activities to use after Lesson 3)

In this activity, students analyze three word problems involving decimals. Each word problem is shown with an incorrect solution. The goal is to have students identify the type of error made as well as the method needed to correct each error. In the Extend It students use what they learned to create a checklist they can use to identify common errors in their own math work.

Math Journal You may wish to have students use their *Math Journals* to answer the Extend It question.

Going Beyond Have students work in pairs to extend the checklist with other possible errors. You may wish to place these on a poster in the classroom for reference.

Solutions

1. *Answers may vary. Sample:* Example A: Computational error. The numbers are not added correctly because the decimal points are aligned incorrectly. Example B: Computational error. The numbers are subtracted incorrectly. Example C: Operational error. The operation used to solve the problem should be addition, not subtraction.
2. *Answers may vary. Sample:* The digits were not aligned correctly. To fix the error, align the digits of each number in their correct place:

$$\begin{array}{r} 123.2 \\ \underline{+\ 23.45} \\ 146.65 \end{array}$$

3. *Answers may vary. Sample:* Write zeros in the decimal places of the whole number so that you can regroup to subtract. Write a decimal point and 2 zeros to the right of 38. Then regroup to subtract:

$$\begin{array}{r} 38.00 \\ \underline{-5.76} \\ 32.24 \end{array}$$

4. *Answers may vary. Sample:* I would look for clue words to help me decide if I should add or subtract. Since Aaron ran 0.8 mile *more* this week than last week, I would add to find the total number of miles. $7.4 + 0.8 = 8.2$. Aaron ran 8.2 miles this week.

Extend It *Answers may vary. Sample checklist:*

- Did I correctly align my decimals?
- Did I write zeros as placeholders and regroup when necessary?
- Did I use the correct operation to solve the problem?

Name ______________________________ Date ____________

Math and Stock Prices

When you buy a share of stock you are buying part of a company. Stock prices move up and down each day. The graph on the right shows the closing price per share of stock for two companies during one week. You can use the graph to see how the stock prices changed from day to day.

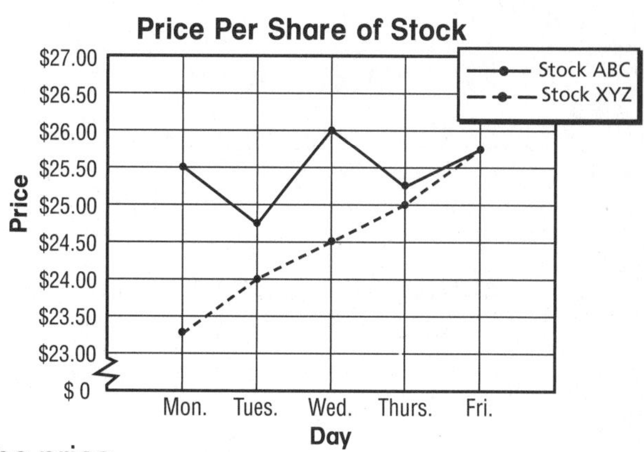

1. **Summarize** Describe the weekly trend of the price per share for both stocks shown on the graph.

____

2. **Predict** If the trend for the stock price of each stock continues during the next week, what price do you predict each stock will have on the next day of trading?

____

3. **Analyze** A grandfather bought his grandchild 2 shares of each stock. The four shares were worth $101.00. On which day did he buy the stock? Explain how you found your answer.

____

4. **Compare and Contrast** Suppose you bought 1 share of each stock for each day shown on the graph. On which stock would you have spent a greater amount? How much more would you have spent on this stock than on the other stock?

____

5. **Explain** Suppose you bought 2 shares of each stock on Monday and sold the shares on Thursday. Would you have a gain or a loss? Explain.

____

Connect It

On a separate sheet of paper, write and solve two word problems about the graph. One word problem should use addition and the other should use subtraction.

Teacher Notes

Connect: Math and Stock Prices

Objective Solve multistep problems about the stock market using addition and subtraction of decimals.

Using the Connect (Activities to use after Lesson 5)
In this activity, students analyze data about the change in prices of two shares of stock over 5 days and solve multistep word problems. The problems require students to use what they have learned about adding and subtracting decimals to interpret and compare the given data. The Connect it challenges students to write their own word problems involving stock prices and addition and subtraction of decimals.

Math Journal You may wish to have students use their *Math Journals* to answer the Connect It question.

Going Beyond Tell students they have an imaginary amount of money to spend on stocks. Have them use a newspaper to choose 2 real stocks to buy at the closing price on a given day. Have them follow the stock prices for a week and sell their stocks on any day they choose. Have students report their profits or losses.

Solutions

1. *Answers may vary. Sample:* Stock ABC follows a pattern of rising and falling on each consecutive day. Stock XYZ rises steadily each day.
2. *Answers may vary. Sample:* ABC: \$25.00; XYZ: \$26.50
3. Wednesday. *Answers may vary. Sample:* I found the share price for each stock each day. Then I multiplied each stock's price by 2. Then I added the prices for the 2 shares of each stock on each day. The price on Wednesday was \$101.00, so I knew he bought the stocks on Wednesday.
4. Stock ABC; \$4.75 more
5. You would have a gain. *Answers may vary. Sample:* You would have lost \$0.50 on stock ABC, but made \$3.50 on stock XYZ, so you would have a total gain of \$3.00 on the shares.

Connect It *Answers may vary. Sample:* Addition: How much would 2 shares of stock ABC cost if you bought it on Friday? (\$51.50) Subtraction: On Wednesday, how much more would a share of stock ABC cost than a share of stock XYZ? (\$1.50 more)

Name ______________________ Date ____________

Fraction Products

The product of two positive whole numbers is always greater than either of its factors. You can explore whether this is true for the product of two fractions.

Find each product. Write each product in simplest form.

1. $\frac{1}{2} \times \frac{3}{4} =$ ______ **2.** $\frac{5}{2} \times 10 =$ ______ **3.** $\frac{8}{7} \times \frac{7}{8} =$ ______

4. $\frac{4}{5} \times \frac{10}{3} =$ ______ **5.** $\frac{3}{5} \times \frac{5}{3} =$ ______ **6.** $\frac{9}{5} \times \frac{4}{9} =$ ______

7. Analyze When is the product of two fractions greater than its factors?

____

____

8. Analyze When is the product of two fractions less than its factors?

____

____

9. Create Write and solve 3 equations using multiplication of fractions. The first product should be greater than 1, the second product should be equal to 1, and the third product should be less than 1.

Product greater than 1: ______________________

Product equal to 1: ______________________

Product less than 1: ______________________

Explore It

How can you tell if the product of two fractions is less than, equal to, or greater than 1? On a separate sheet of paper, explain your answer.

Teacher Notes

Explore: Fraction Products

Objective Use patterns to predict the product of two fractions.

Using the Explore (Activities to use after Lesson 2)

The product of two positive whole numbers (other than 1 and 0) is always greater than its factors. This rule does not apply to the product of fractions, a concept that can be challenging. In this activity, students look at the product of fractions to discover patterns that indicate when the product will be greater than its factors, less than its factors, greater than 1, less than 1, or equal to 1.

Math Journal You may wish to have students use their *Math Journals* to answer the Explore It question.

Going Beyond Have students consider an algebraic representation of the patterns they have found. Pose the question: When is $\frac{a}{b} \times \frac{c}{d}$ greater than, less than, or equal to 1? $\frac{a}{b} \times \frac{c}{d}$ is greater than 1 when $ac > bd$. $\frac{a}{b} \times \frac{c}{d}$ is less than 1 when $ac < bd$. $ac = bd$ when $\frac{a}{b} \times \frac{c}{d} = 1$.

Solutions

1. $\frac{3}{8}$
2. 25
3. 1
4. $2\frac{2}{3}$
5. 1
6. $\frac{4}{5}$
7. *Answers may vary. Sample:* The product of two fractions is greater than one of its factors when one of the factors is greater than 1. The product of two fractions is greater than both of its factors when both of the factors are greater than 1.
8. The product of two fractions is less than its factors when both factors are less than 1.
9. *Answers may vary. Sample:* $\frac{5}{4} \times \frac{3}{2} = \frac{15}{8} = 1\frac{7}{8}$; $\frac{7}{2} \times \frac{2}{7} = \frac{14}{14} = 1$; $\frac{1}{4} \times \frac{4}{5} = \frac{4}{20} = \frac{1}{5}$

Explore It *Answers may vary. Sample:* You can look at the numerators and denominators of the fractions. The product is less than 1 if the product of the numerators is less than the product of the denominators. The product is greater than 1 if the product of the numerators is greater than the product of the denominators. The product is equal to 1 if the product of the numerators is equal to the product of the denominators.

Name ______________________ Date __________

Use Fractions to Compare

The circle graphs below show the results of a survey conducted by a young children's magazine. Two hundred first graders, 400 second graders, and 600 third graders were asked which type of pet they prefer.

Favorite Pets

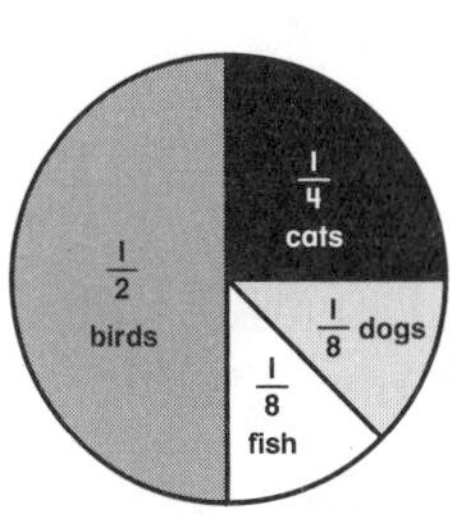

200 First Graders

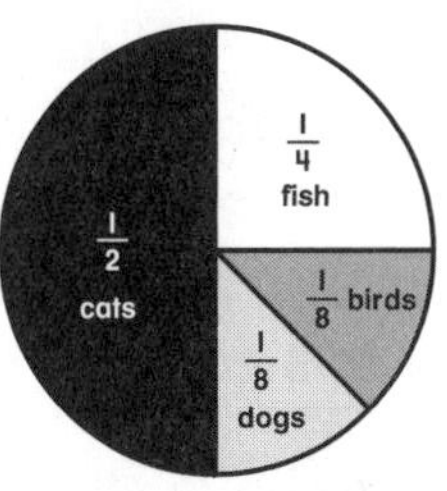

400 Second Graders

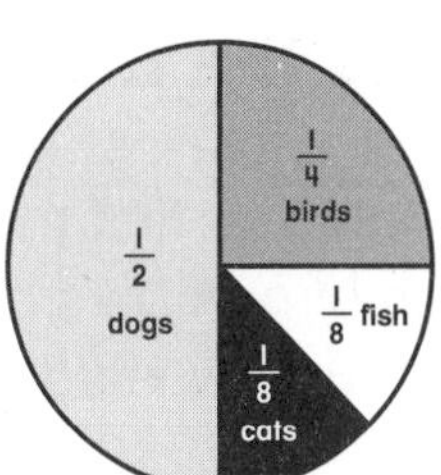

600 Third Graders

Use the circle graphs to complete the tables below.

First Graders' Favorite Pets		
Type of pet	Fraction of students	Number of students
Dogs		
Cats		
Birds		
Fish		

Second Graders' Favorite Pets		
Type of pet	Fraction of students	Number of students
Dogs		
Cats		
Birds		
Fish		

Third Graders' Favorite Pets		
Type of pet	Fraction of students	Number of students
Dogs		
Cats		
Birds		
Fish		

1. **Compare** Which type of pet is preferred by the greatest number of students? How many students prefer this pet? Explain.

____

____

2. What fraction of each grade prefers that pet? ______________________

____

Extend It

One-half of first graders and $\frac{1}{4}$ of third graders prefer birds. One-half is greater than $\frac{1}{4}$, yet more third graders than first graders prefer birds. On a separate sheet of paper, explain how this can be true.

Teacher Notes

Extend: Use Fractions to Compare

Objective Use fractions to compare.

Using the Extend (Activities to use after Lesson 3)

In this activity, students discover that in order to compare parts of a whole you first must consider the size of the whole. A survey of different numbers of first, second, and third graders illustrates this point. Finally, students apply this concept to a particular situation.

Math Journal You may wish to have students use their *Math Journals* to answer the Extend It.

Going Beyond Have students give examples of other situations where $\frac{1}{2}$ of a group results in a lesser number than $\frac{1}{4}$ of a different group.

Solutions

First Graders' Favorite Pets		
Type of Pet	Fraction of students	Number of students
Dogs	$\frac{1}{8}$	25
Cats	$\frac{1}{4}$	50
Birds	$\frac{1}{2}$	100
Fish	$\frac{1}{8}$	25

Second Graders' Favorite Pets		
Type of Pet	Fraction of students	Number of students
Dogs	$\frac{1}{8}$	50
Cats	$\frac{1}{2}$	200
Birds	$\frac{1}{8}$	50
Fish	$\frac{1}{4}$	100

Third Graders' Favorite Pets		
Type of Pet	Fraction of students	Number of students
Dogs	$\frac{1}{2}$	300
Cats	$\frac{1}{8}$	75
Birds	$\frac{1}{4}$	150
Fish	$\frac{1}{8}$	75

1. The dog is preferred by the greatest number of students. I found this by multiplying the fraction of students in each grade by the number of students in each grade and then adding the results. 375 students prefer dogs.
2. $\frac{1}{8}$ of first graders, $\frac{1}{8}$ of second graders and $\frac{1}{2}$ of third graders prefer dogs.

Extend It *Answers may vary. Sample:* This can be true because there are a greater number of third graders than first graders. $\frac{1}{4}$ of 600 third graders is 150 third graders. $\frac{1}{2}$ of 200 first graders is 100 first graders.

Name ______________________ Date __________

Fraction Division

You have learned to divide fractions by multiplying by the reciprocal of the divisor. There is another way to divide fractions.

Find $\frac{3}{4} \div \frac{1}{2}$.

Find the least common denominator, 4. Rewrite each fraction as an equivalent fraction using the LCD. $\frac{3}{4} \div \frac{2}{4}$	Place the numerator of the dividend in the numerator of the quotient. Place the numerator of the divisor in the denominator of the quotient. $\frac{3}{4} \div \frac{2}{4} = \frac{3}{2}$	Simplify. $\frac{3}{2} = 1\frac{1}{2}$

Use this method to find each quotient. Show your work.

1. $\frac{4}{5} \div \frac{5}{8} =$ ______ **2.** $\frac{7}{12} \div \frac{8}{12} =$ ______

3. $\frac{2}{3} \div \frac{3}{4} =$ ______ **4.** $\frac{3}{7} \div \frac{1}{3} =$ ______

5. Explain Which method is easier to use when you divide fractions with like denominators? Explain. ______

6. Compare Which method of dividing fractions do you prefer? Explain your reasoning. ______

Connect It

On a separate sheet of paper, draw a model for Exercise 3 that illustrates this method of dividing fractions. Use your model to explain this method.

Teacher Notes

Connect: Fraction Division

Objective Use the common denominator algorithm to divide fractions.

Using the Connect (Activities to use after Lesson 5)

In this chapter, students have learned to divide fractions by multiplying by the reciprocal of the divisor. In this activity, students explore an alternative algorithm in which they first find a common denominator and then divide the numerators. This algorithm may be more intuitive for most students, however it is not as efficient. Students explain how this algorithm works and decide which algorithm they prefer to use.

Math Journal You may wish to have students use their *Math Journals* to answer the Connect It.

Going Beyond Have students explain why the invert and multiply method of division works. Explanations should include an understanding of reciprocals.

Solutions

1. $\frac{4}{5} \div \frac{5}{8}$ $\quad \frac{32}{40} \div \frac{25}{40}$ $\quad \frac{32}{25} = 1\frac{7}{25}$
2. $\frac{7}{12} \div \frac{8}{12} = \frac{7}{8}$
3. $\frac{2}{3} \div \frac{3}{4}$ $\quad \frac{8}{12} \div \frac{9}{12}$ $\quad \frac{8}{9}$
4. $\frac{3}{7} \div \frac{1}{3}$ $\quad \frac{9}{21} \div \frac{7}{21}$ $\quad \frac{9}{7} = 1\frac{2}{7}$
5. *Answers may vary. Sample:* The alternate method is easier to use. You do not need to multiply.
6. *Answers may vary. Sample:* I prefer the method where you multiply by the reciprocal because it is easier to use. When the fractions already have the same denominator, I prefer to use the alternate method. Then this method is easier to use.

Connect It *Answers may vary. Sample:*

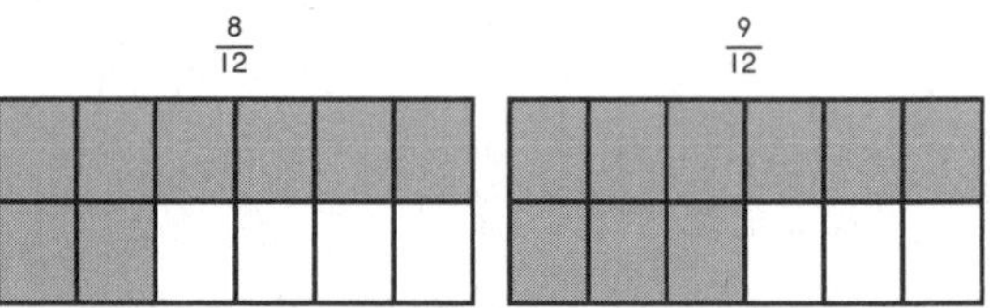

First rewrite $\frac{2}{3}$ as $\frac{8}{12}$, and $\frac{3}{4}$ as $\frac{9}{12}$. Then find how many $\frac{9}{12}$ are in $\frac{8}{12}$. You can see that 8 out of 9 twelfths fit in $\frac{8}{12}$, so the quotient is $\frac{8}{9}$. By finding the common denominator, you make the sections in the model the same size. Once they are the same size, it is only the numerators that need be considered.

Name ______________________ Date ____________

Relate Multiplication and Division

Did you know that you can use division to help you multiply a whole number by a decimal less than 1?

Solve

$120 \times 0.5 =$ ______ $120 \div 2 =$ ______

1. **Compare** Which numbers are in both of these number sentences? How are these numbers used differently in the two equations?

____

2. **Analyze** Write 0.5 as a fraction in simplest form. ______________
What do you notice about the denominator of this fraction and the divisor in the division sentence above? ______________

____

Find each product. Then write a related division sentence for each multiplication sentence.

3. $120 \times 0.1 =$ ______ Division Sentence: ______________
4. $120 \times 0.2 =$ ______ Division Sentence: ______________
5. $40 \times 0.5 =$ ______ Division Sentence: ______________
6. $40 \times 0.25 =$ ______ Division Sentence: ______________
7. $50 \times 0.1 =$ ______ Division Sentence: ______________
8. $50 \times 0.2 =$ ______ Division Sentence: ______________
9. $60 \times 0.25 =$ ______ Division Sentence: ______________
10. $60 \times 0.5 =$ ______ Division Sentence: ______________

Explore It

Can you use division to help you multiply 120 by 0.125? On a separate sheet of paper, explain why or why not.

Teacher Notes

Explore: Relate Multiplication and Division

Objective Use division of whole numbers to find the product of decimals.

Using the Explore (Activities to use after Lesson 2)

In this activity, students explore the relationship between multiplication and division. Students multiply whole numbers by tenths and hundredths decimals. Students are guided to understand that multiplying a number by 0.5 is the same as dividing that number by 2. Students then use this relationship between multiplication and division to find products and write related division sentences. In the Explore It, students use this relationship to find a product of a whole number and a thousandths decimal.

Math Journal You may wish to have students use their *Math Journals* to answer the Explore It question.

Going Beyond Have students explore this relationship with other decimals. Students should discover that this relationship only holds true for decimals that can be written as unit fractions.

Solutions

60; 60

1. 120, 60; *Answer may vary. Sample:* 120 is a factor in the multiplication sentence and the dividend in the division sentence. 60 is the product in the multiplication sentence and the quotient in the division sentence.
2. $\frac{1}{2}$; *Answer may vary. Sample:* The denominator, 2, is equal to the divisor, 2, in the division problem.
3. 12; $120 \div 10 = 12$
4. 24; $120 \div 5 = 24$
5. 20; $40 \div 2 = 20$
6. 10; $40 \div 4 = 10$
7. 5; $50 \div 10 = 5$
8. 10; $50 \div 5 = 10$
9. 15; $60 \div 4 = 15$
10. 30; $60 \div 2 = 30$

Explore It *Answers may vary. Sample:* Yes. 0.125 can be written as the fraction $\frac{125}{1,000}$. This simplifies to $\frac{1}{8}$. The related division sentence is $120 \div 8$. $120 \div 8 = 15$, so $120 \times 0.125 = 15$.

Name ______________________ Date __________

Converting Measurements

Many countries other than the United States use metric measurement. To convert from a unit of measure in the first column of the table to a unit of measure in the second column, multiply by the conversion factor.

Unit of Measure	Unit of Measure	Conversion Factor
kilometers	miles	0.6214
miles	kilometers	1.6093
liters	gallons	0.2642
gallons	liters	3.7853
kilograms	pounds	2.2046
pounds	kilograms	0.4536

Use the table and a calculator to find each measurement.

1. 60 kilometers = _____ miles

2. 85 miles = _____ kilometers

3. 2 liters = _____ gallons

4. 1 gallon = _____ liters

5. 50 kilograms = _____ pounds

6. 120 pounds = _____ kilograms

7. **Analyze** Look at the table above. Explain how you can tell which length is greater, 1 kilometer or 1 mile.

____

8. **Explain** An airline has a weight limit of 40 pounds for each piece of luggage. Suppose your luggage weighs 20 kilograms. Is your luggage too heavy? Explain your answer.

____

Extend It

How could you make these conversions easier to use? Describe ways you could use estimation and mental math to convert between customary and metric measurements.

Teacher Notes

Extend: Converting Measurements

Objective Use estimation to convert between customary and metric measures.
Materials calculator

Using the Extend (Activities to use after Lesson 3)

In this activity, students discover ways to use multiplication and estimation to convert between customary and metric measures. Using a conversion table and a calculator, they first find the exact conversions and then create their own estimation techniques. By rounding and converting decimals to fractions they further explore the relationship between fractions and decimals.

Math Journal You may wish to have students use their *Math Journals* to answer the Extend It question.

Going Beyond Have students look at the relationship between conversion factors when converting back and forth between customary and metric measures. Students will find that when going back and forth they are multiplying by the reciprocal of the conversion factor.

Solution

1. 60 kilometers = 37.284 miles
2. 85 miles = 136.7905 kilometers
3. 2 liters = 0.5284 gallons
4. 1 gallon = 3.7853 liters
5. 50 kilograms = 110.23 pounds
6. 120 pounds = 54.432 kilograms
7. *Answers may vary. Sample:* You can tell that 1 mile is the greater length because the conversion factor you use to convert from miles to kilometers is greater than 1.
8. *Answers may vary. Sample:* No. I converted kilograms to pounds using the conversion factor 2.2046 from the table. 20 kilograms = 44.092 pounds. The luggage is too heavy.

Extend It *Answers may vary. Sample:* You could make these conversions easier by rounding and estimating answers. To convert kilometers to miles, divide by 2 and then add $\frac{1}{10}$ of the original amount. To convert miles to kilometers, add $\frac{1}{2}$ the original amount and then add $\frac{1}{10}$ of the original amount. To convert liters to gallons, divide by 4. To convert gallons to liters, multiply by 3 and then add $\frac{3}{4}$ of the original amount. To convert kilograms to pounds, multiply by 2 and then add $\frac{1}{5}$ of the original amount. To convert pounds to kilograms, divide by 2 and then subtract $\frac{1}{20}$ of the original amount.

Name ______________________ Date __________

Decimal Movement

Looking at patterns in the movement of the decimal point can help you estimate decimal products.

Multiply to complete the table below.

×	800	80	8	0.8	0.08	0.008
400						
40						
4						
0.4						
0.04						
0.004						

1. **Interpret** Describe the patterns you see in the table.

____

____

____

2. Use the patterns you found in the table to complete the multiplication sentences.

a. 8,000 × 4,000 = ______

80,000 × ______ = ______

______ × ______ = ______

b. 0.0004 × 0.0008 = ______

0.00004 × ______ = ______

______ × ______ = ______

Connect It

On a separate sheet of paper, explain how you can use the patterns you found in the table to help you multiply decimals.

Teacher Notes

Connect: Decimal Movement

Objective Use multiplication to find products and patterns.

Using the Connect (Activities to use after Lesson 5)

The location of the decimal point in a product depends on the location of the decimal points in the factors. Students explore multiplication of the factors 8 and 4 with shifting powers of ten in different combinations. The Connect It helps students discover ways to use mental math to help them find the products of decimal factors.

Math Journal You may wish to have students use their *Math Journals* to answer the Connect It question.

Going Beyond Have students explore different relationships by making up their own tables with different numbers.

Solutions

×	**800**	**80**	**8**	**0.8**	**0.08**	**0.008**
400	320,000	32,000	3,200	320	32	3.2
40	32,000	3,200	320	32	3.2	0.32
4	3,200	320	32	3.2	0.32	0.032
0.4	320	32	3.2	0.32	0.032	0.0032
0.04	32	3.2	0.32	0.032	0.0032	0.00032
0.004	3.2	0.32	0.032	0.0032	0.00032	0.000032

1. *Answers may vary. Sample:* All the products contain the product of the basic fact $4 \times 8 = 32$. As you go down a column, the product decreases by a power of ten. As you go across each row, the product decreases by a power of ten.
2. *Answers may vary depending on students' patterns. Sample:*
   a. 32,000,000; 40,000; 3,200,000,000; 800,000; 400,000; 320,000,000,000
   b. *Answers may vary depending on students' patterns. Sample:* 0.00000032 0.00008; 0.0000000032 0.000004; 0.000008; 0.000000000032

Connect It *Answers may vary. Sample:* When multiplying decimals, first find the product of the basic fact, then move the decimal point to the left based on the place value of the factors.

Name ______________________ Date ____________

Divisor/Quotient Relationships

Dividing with decimals is similar to dividing with whole numbers, but it also can produce some interesting results. This is especially true when you divide by numbers less than 1.

1. Start with simple division using whole numbers. Find these quotients.

$60 \div 5 =$ ______ $60 \div 4 =$ ______ $60 \div 3 =$ ______

$60 \div 2 =$ ______ $60 \div 1 =$ ______

2. As the divisors decrease, what do you notice about the quotients in Exercise 1?

____

3. In Exercise 1, are the quotients greater than or less than the dividend? ____________

4. Use your calculator to find these quotients.

$60 \div 0.5 =$ ______ $60 \div 0.4 =$ ______ $60 \div 0.3 =$ ______

$60 \div 0.2 =$ ______ $60 \div 0.1 =$ ______

5. **Compare** How are the quotients in Exercise 4 different from the quotients in Exercise 1?

____

6. Now use the same dividend but divide with a lesser decimal divisor.

$60 \div 0.05 =$ ______ $60 \div 0.04 =$ ______ $60 \div 0.03 =$ ______

$60 \div 0.02 =$ ______ $60 \div 0.01 =$ ______

7. What can you say about the relationship between quotients and dividends when your divisor is less than 1? ______________________

Explore It

Do you think there are any limits to the relationship between quotients and dividends? On a separate sheet of paper, explain why or why not.

Teacher Notes

Explore: Divisor/Quotient Relationships

Objective Explore the relationship between decimal divisors and quotient size.
Materials calculator

Using the Explore (Activities to use after Lesson 1)

Using whole numbers, students become familiar with the fact that as divisors decrease, quotients increase. Divisors less than 1 not only continue this pattern, but can lead to surprising results—namely, quotients that are larger than the dividend. Since there is no limit to how small a decimal divisor can be, quotients can increase without limit as well. Students investigate the nature of this relationship between dividends, quotients, and divisors less than 1. In the Explore It students consider whether or not the relationship has limits.

Math Journal You may wish to have students use their *Math Journals* to answer the Explore It question.

Going Beyond Encourage students to further experiment with the results of dividing numbers by decimals less than 1. Suggest that they experiment with dividing decimals less than 1 by other decimals less than 1. Have them find the largest and smallest quotients they can.

Solutions

1. 12; 15; 20; 30; 60
2. As the divisors decrease, the quotients increase.
3. Less than the dividend
4. 120; 150; 200; 300; 600
5. Each quotient in Exercise 4 is 10 times greater than each quotient in Exercise 1.
6. 1,200; 1,500; 2,000; 3,000; 6,000
7. *Answers may vary. Sample:* As the divisor decreases, the quotient increases. When the divisor is less than 1, the quotient is greater than the dividend.

Explore It *Answers may vary. Sample:* No, because you can continue to use lesser decimals as dividends. That means that the quotients will continue to increase.

Name ______________________ Date __________

Powers of 10

One use for multiplying and dividing by powers of 10 is in the metric system. The metric system is based on powers of 10. You can change between metric units by multiplying and dividing by powers of ten.

For example, multiply by 10^3 to find the number of grams in 1 kilogram. $1 \times 10^3 = 1{,}000$. So 1 kilogram = 1,000 grams.

Other measurements can involve much greater powers of 10. You can identify the powers of 10 by looking for the prefix in each measurement.

Prefix	Value
giga-	1,000,000,000
mega-	1,000,000
kilo-	1,000
(none)	1
milli-	0.001
micro-	0.000001
nano-	0.000000001

Use the table to answer the following questions.

1. How does the value of each number in the chart compare to the number below it? ______________________

2. **Analyze** If a measurement is given in meters, by what power of 10 do you have to multiply to change to megameters? ______________________

Write and solve an equation using powers of 10 to answer each question.

3. The average distance from Earth to the moon is about 384,000 kilometers. What is this distance in gigameters?

____

4. A speck of dust is 512 micrometers in length. How long is this in megameters? ______________________

Extend It

When changing units of measurement, why is it helpful to multiply and divide by powers of 10? On a separate sheet of paper, explain your answer.

Teacher Notes

Extend: Powers of 10

Objective Extend multiplication and division by powers of ten to change between metric measurements.

Using the Extend (Activities to use after Lesson 3)

In Lesson 3 of this chapter, students learn how to multiply and divide by powers of 10 through 10^3. The units of the metric system offer students an opportunity to extend this skill. Since the metric system has unit prefixes ranging from atto- (10^{-18}) to exa- (10^{18}), students can use their knowledge to solve problems that involve greater powers of ten. The Extend It asks students to analyze the usefulness of a measurement system based on multiplying and dividing by powers of ten.

Math Journal You may wish to have students use their *Math Journals* to answer the Extend It question.

Going Beyond Have students look for examples of metric measurements in books, newspapers, and real-life objects. Then ask them to change these to other metric measurement by multiplying and dividing by powers of ten.

Solutions

1. Each number is 1,000 times greater than the number below it.
2. 10^6
3. $384{,}000 \div 10^6 = 0.384$ gigameters
4. $512 \div 10^{12} = .000000000512$ megameters

Extend It *Answers may vary. Sample:* It is helpful because you can change from one unit to another by looking at each unit's prefix. Then you can decide which way to move the decimal point.

Name ________________________________ Date ____________

Decimal Division

Softball uses decimal division to show important statistics. The batting average divides the number of hits that a player gets by the number of times he or she has come up to bat. Use your calculator to complete the batting average table below. Round your answers as necessary.

Sports statistics often drop the leading zero in decimals less than 1.

	Player	Hits	At-Bats	Batting Average
1.	Moro	89	244	______
2.	Diaz	52	______	.263
3.	McGregor	______	55	.327

4. Explain What is the greatest possible batting average? Explain how you know.

____

An important pitching statistic is winning percentage. This divides the number of games a pitcher has won by the pitcher's total number of wins and losses. Complete the win-loss table below.

	Pitcher	Wins	Losses	Percentage
5.	Okwu	4	______	.308
6.	Veloso	7	______	.538

7. Explain how you found the number of games lost by pitcher Okwu.

____

Connect It

Suppose that a player bats .500 or a pitcher has a 1.000 winning percentage. Does this mean that the player is a good hitter or pitcher? Do you need more information about the player? On a separate piece of paper, explain your answer and support it with an example.

Teacher Notes

Connect: Decimal Division

Objective Investigate how decimal division can be applied to sports statistics.

Using the Connect (Activities to use after Lesson 5)

Sports statistics offer a familiar example of the use of decimals in division. In this activity, students use fictitious softball statistics to apply their knowledge of dividing decimals. The Connect It gives students a chance to evaluate the usefulness of decimal statistics in sports.

Math Journal You may wish to have students use their *Math Journals* to answer the Connect It question.

Going Beyond Have students research softball, baseball, or other sports statistics in the newspaper or online. Then have them use these real-life statistics to write decimal division word problems.

Solutions

1. .365

2. 198

3. 18

4. 1.000, or 1. *Answers may vary. Sample:* The greatest possible number of hits is equal to the number of at-bats. Dividing these numbers results in a quotient of 1.

5. 9

6. 6

7. *Answers may vary. Sample:* I divided 4 by .308 to find the total number of wins and losses. $4 \div .308 = 12.98$. I rounded 12.98 to 13 wins and losses. Then I subtracted 4 wins from 13 wins and losses to find 9 losses.

Connect It *Answers may vary. Sample:* No. The player may not be a good hitter or pitcher. The pitcher may have won 1 game and lost 0 games, or the batter may have come up to bat twice and gotten 1 hit. The statistic may be based on a small number of games or at-bats, so it may not be a good indicator of the player's skill.

Name ______________________ Date ____________

Investigate Points and Lines

You may be used to thinking of a point as a small dot. You may also think of a line as a thin black stretch of ink with arrows at each end. These images help us understand geometric ideas, but do the images fit the geometric definitions?

1. Use a metric ruler to measure this drawing of a point.

   What is its diameter? ______________________

2. This square measures 2 cm × 2 cm. About how many copies of the drawing of a point can fit in the box?

   ____

3. According to the rules of geometry, points have no width or length. What does that suggest about the above drawing of a point? ______________________

4. The rules of geometry also state that lines and line segments have length, but no width. Use a metric ruler to measure and record the length of this line segment.

   ____

   Does the line segment have a width? ______________

5. Draw the smallest point and thinnest line that you can.

6. Do your drawings of a point and line meet the definitions of a point and a line?

   Why or why not? ______________________

   ____

Explore It

Could you see a one-dimensional line? On a separate sheet of paper, explain why for why not.

Teacher Notes

Explore: Investigate Points and Lines

Objective Explore the differences between the concepts of points and lines and their graphical representations.
Materials centimeter ruler

Using the Explore (Activities to use after Lesson 1)

Students are most familiar with geometric points and lines through their graphical representations. However, these representations show points, lines, and rays as two-dimensional objects, when in fact they are one- or no-dimensional. In this activity, students are encouraged to deepen their understandings of points and lines by contrasting each concept with its graphical representation. In the Explore It, students are asked to consider the visibility of a one-dimensional object.

Math Journal You may wish to have students use their *Math Journals* to answer the Explore It question.

Going Beyond Ask students whether they can think of any changes that would improve the graphical representations of points and lines. Encourage them to consider both the accuracy and usefulness of each representation.

Solutions

1. 2 millimeters
2. about 100 copies of the drawing of a point
3. *Answers may vary. Sample:* It is not really a point, because it has a diameter. It is a representation of a point.
4. 4 centimeters; yes
5. *Students' drawings should show a very small point and very thin line.*
6. *Answers may vary. Sample:* No, because the drawing of a point still has a very small length and width, and the drawing of the line still has a very small width.

Explore It *Answers may vary. Sample:* No, because if the line was one-dimensional, it would have no width at all. You would not be able to draw it or see it.

Name ________________________ Date ____________

The Pythagorean Theorem

Pythagoras was a Greek mathematician and philosopher who lived about 2,500 years ago. He is credited with discovering an important fact about right triangles.

Look at the right triangle at right. Sides *a* and *b* form a right angle. Across from the right angle is side *c*. The Pythagorean theorem states that $a^2 + b^2 = c^2$.

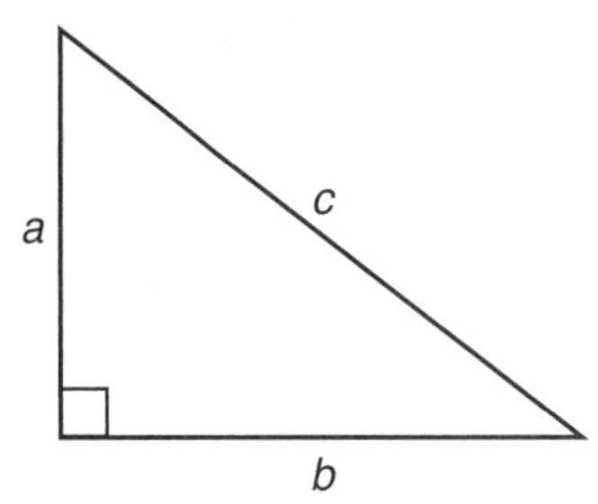

1. A right triangle has sides 3 cm, 4 cm, and 5 cm. Apply the Pythagorean theorem to the triangle.

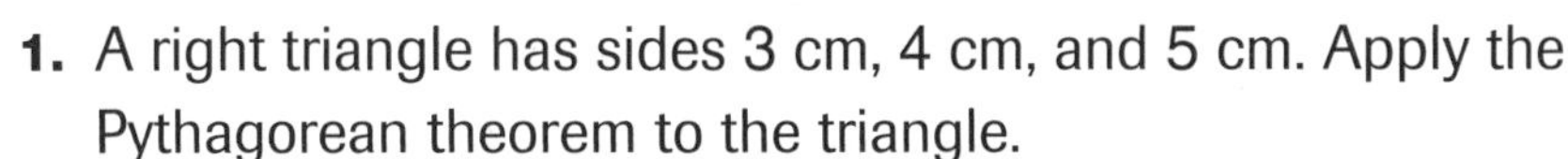

____

2. You can verify visually that the Pythagorean theorem is true. In the right triangle at right, a 3×3 grid has been extended from the 3 cm side of the triangle to represent 3^2. Since $3^2 = 9$, there are 9 square cm boxes. Draw similar grids for the 4 cm side and the 5 cm side of the triangle.

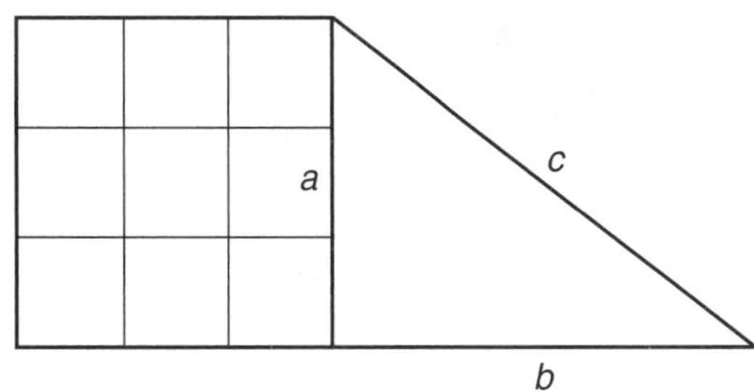

3. **Analyze** How do the square grids verify that the Pythagorean theorem is true?

____

4. Look at the right triangle at right. The square of side *a* is 25. The square of side *b* is 144. What is the length of side *c*? Explain how you found your answer.

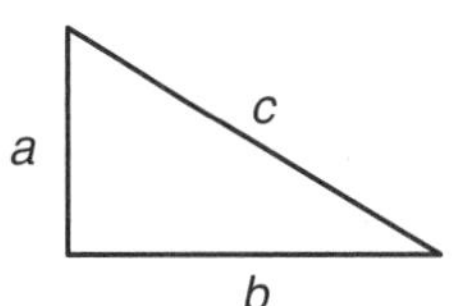

____

____

Extend It

On a separate sheet of paper, write a word problem that uses the Pythagorean theorem. Be sure to include your answer.

Teacher Notes

Extend: The Pythagorean Theorem

Objective Increase understanding of triangles by learning about the Pythagorean theorem.

Using the Extend (Activities to use after Lesson 3)

In this activity, students are introduced to the Pythagorean theorem. They use the theorem to identify the length of the hypotenuse of a right triangle, and apply their knowledge of squaring small numbers. The Extend It encourages students to create a word problem that uses the Pythagorean theorem.

Math Journal You may wish to have students use their *Math Journals* to answer the Extend It.

Going Beyond Have students research Pythagoras and his followers. Have them present their findings in a short oral report.

Solutions

1. $3^2 + 4^2 = 5^2$; $9 + 16 = 25$

2.

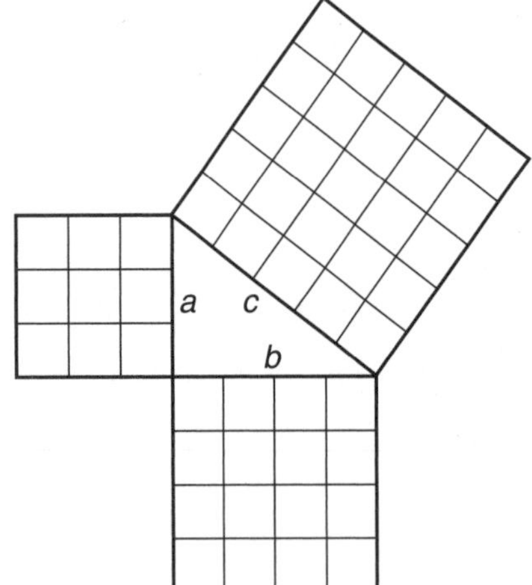

3. The number of squares for side *a*, 9, plus the number of squares for side *b*, 16, equals the number of squares for side *c*, 25.

4. 9; *Answers may vary. Sample:* I use the Pythagorean theorem, $a^2 + b^2 = c^2$. $25 + 144 = c^2$; $169 = c^2$; $13 = c$. The length of side *c* is 13.

Extend It *Answers may vary. Sample:* A pane of glass is shaped like a right triangle. Side *a* is 6 feet long, and side *b* is 8 feet long. How long is side *c*? (Answer: 10 feet)

Name ______________________ Date __________

Analyze a Street Map

Street maps can do more than just show how to get from one place to another. They also show examples of polygons. Look at this section of a map of Washington, D.C.

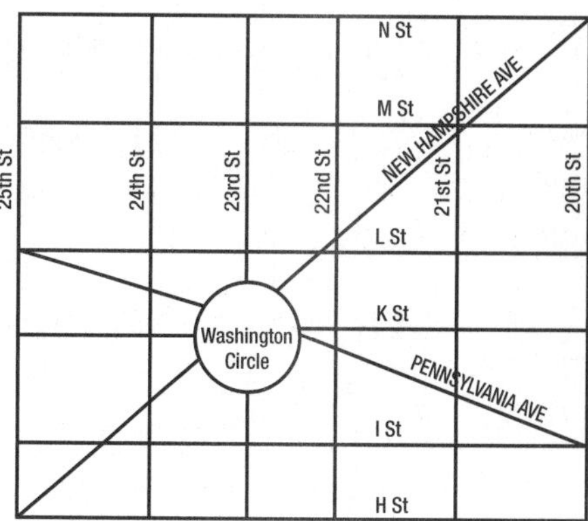

1. **Analyze** There are two sets of parallel streets. What is the system used for naming them?

____

____

Each of the polygons in Exercises 2–4 can be found on the map. Find one example of each, and list the streets that form the sides of the polygon.

2. rectangle ______________________

3. trapezoid ______________________

4. triangle ______________________

5. Which location shown on the map is not a polygon? ______________________

6. Suppose you are taking a walk. Follow the directions.
   - **a.** Start walking south from the corner of M Street and 23rd Street.
   - **b.** Turn west on L Street.
   - **c.** Go south on 24th Street.
   - **d.** Turn northwest on Pennsylvania Avenue.
   - **e.** Turn north onto 25th Street.
   - **f.** Go east onto M Street until you return to your starting point.

   What figure is outlined by the path you traveled? ______________________

Connect It

Draw the block formed by K and L streets and 24th and 25th streets. Then draw the diagonal. Which line or lines do you think are the longest? Explain your reasoning.

Teacher Notes

Connect: Analyze a Street Map

Objective Use a street map to identify polygons by their features, including parallel and perpendicular sides.

Using the Connect (Activities to use after Lesson 5)

The lines of a city street map can form multiple polygons, including squares, rectangles, parallelograms, and triangles. In this activity, students use a map detail of Washington D.C. to identify polygons and the relationships of the lines that form them. The Connect It asks students to compare the length of a quadrilateral's diagonal to the length of its sides.

Math Journal You may wish to have students use their *Math Journals* to answer the Connect It question.

Going Beyond Have students look at a map of your town or city and identify the polygons they find. Which polygons are most common? Which are hard to find?

Solutions

1. One set of parallel streets is named with letters, and the other set is named with numbers.
2. *Answers may vary. Sample:* H Street, 21st Street, I street, and 22nd Street
3. *Answers may vary. Sample:* I Street, New Hampshire Avenue, H Street, and 24th Street
4. *Answers may vary. Sample:* K Street, 25th Street, and Pennsylvania Avenue
5. Washington Circle
6. Hexagon

Connect It

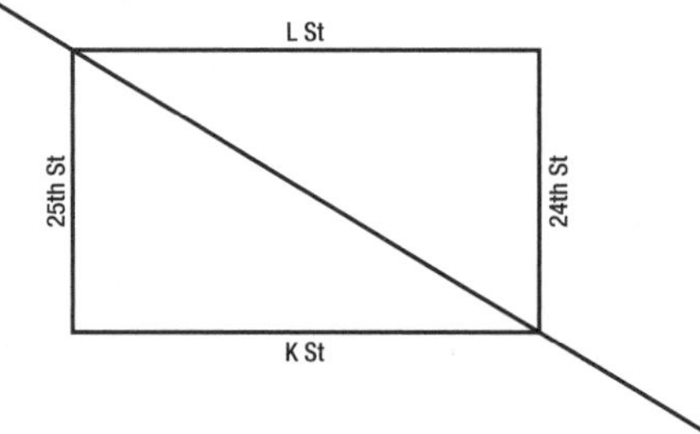

Answers may vary. Sample: I think the diagonal line is the longest. The intersection of 25th Street and K Street forms a right angle. I know that the length of the side opposite the right angle will be the longest side of a right triangle. So I know that the diagonal line is the longest.

Name ______________________________ Date ____________

Investigate Perimeter

Every polygon has exactly one perimeter. A polygon has fixed sides and its perimeter is the sum of the lengths of all the sides. Different polygons can have the same perimeter. Look at the two quadrilaterals to the right.

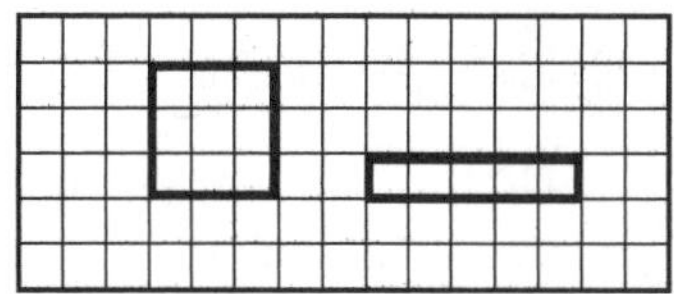

1. Suppose each square unit on the grid has a side length of 1 unit.

   What is the perimeter of the square? ______ units the rectangle? ______ units

For each given perimeter, draw three different squares or rectangles on the grid below.

2. $P = 16$ units
3. $P = 20$ units
4. $P = 26$ units

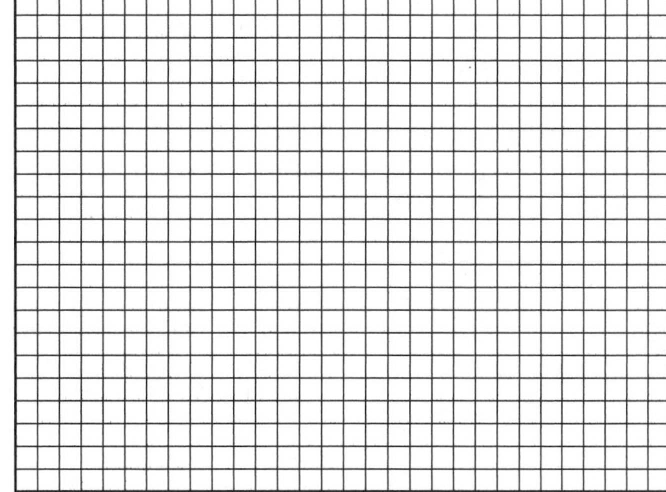

5. **Analyze** Using only whole units, is it possible to draw a square or rectangle with a perimeter of 15 units on the grid? Use perimeter formulas to support your answer. ______________________________

   ____

Explore It

Each square unit on the grid has an area equal to 1 square unit. Find the areas of the quadrilaterals you drew. Which quadrilaterals in each exercise have the greatest area? Which have the least area? Write your results on a separate sheet of paper.

Teacher Notes

Explore: Investigate Perimeter

Objective Explore perimeter by drawing multiple quadrilaterals with equal perimeters.

Using the Explore (Activities to use after Lesson 1)

Every polygon has a fixed perimeter. For a given value of perimeter, many different polygons can be drawn. In this activity, students explore the concept of perimeter by using grid paper to draw sets of quadrilaterals with a given perimeter. In the Explore It students find and compare the areas of the quadrilaterals they drew.

Math Journal You may wish to have students use their *Math Journals* to answer the Explore It questions.

Going Beyond Give students perimeters in inches or centimeters. Then have them use rulers to draw several polygons of different shapes that have the same perimeter.

Solutions

1. 12 units; 12 units
2. *Answers may vary. Sample:*

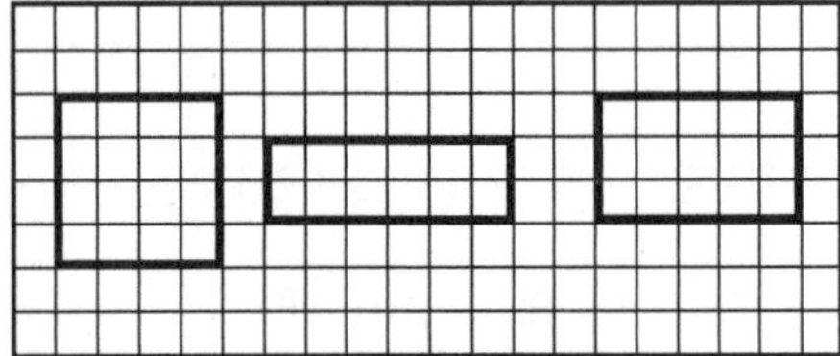

3. *Answers may vary. Sample:*

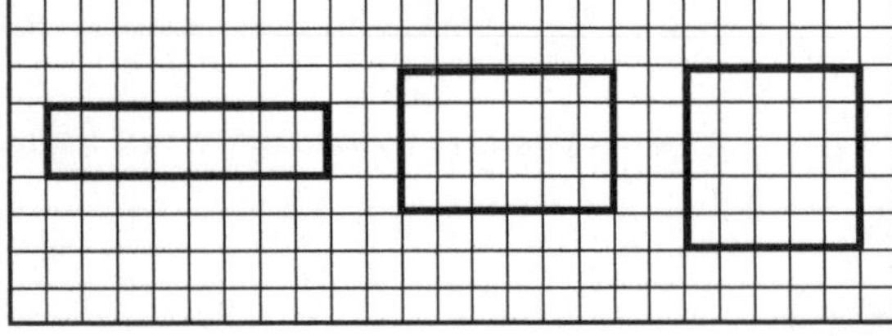

4. *Answers may vary. Sample:*

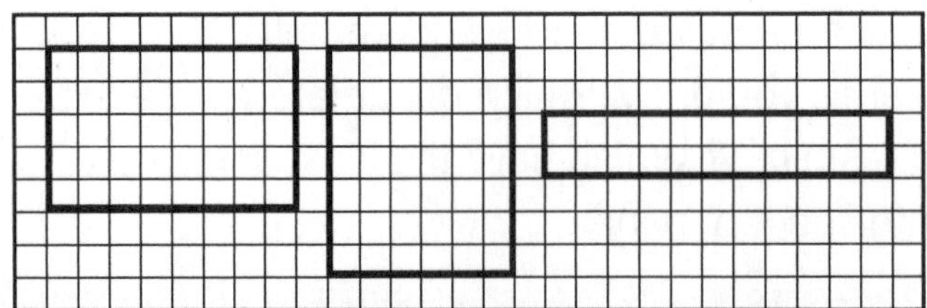

5. No. It is not possible. *Answers may vary. Sample:* The formula for the perimeter of a square is $P = 4s$. If $P = 15$ units, then s, the length of a side, cannot be a whole number because 15 is not evenly divisible by 4. The formula for perimeter of a rectangle is $P = 2l + 2w$, or $P = 2(l + w)$. If $P = 15$ units, then the length and the width of the rectangle cannot both be whole numbers.

Explore It *Answers may vary. Check students' work. Sample:* The quadrilaterals that were squares or close to squares in shape had the greatest area. The thin, long rectangles had the least area.

Name ______________________ Date __________

Estimate Area

Did you know that you can estimate the area of items shown on a map? You can use an approach similar to the one you use to find the area of an irregular polygon. First you draw triangles and rectangles to cover the item on the map. Then you find the area of each polygon and then find the sum of the areas of the polygons.

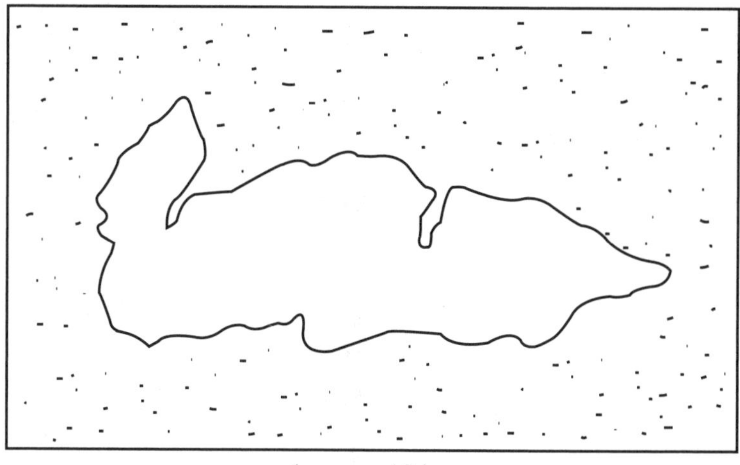

1 cm = 10 km

Look at the map of the island.

1. Use a ruler or a straight edge to draw rectangles and triangles to cover most of the island.

2. Use a centimeter ruler to measure the dimensions of each polygon you drew. Then apply the formulas for the area of a rectangle and the area of a triangle. Write the name and area of each polygon in square centimeters.

   ____

3. **Infer** How many square kilometers does each square centimeter on the map represent? ______________________________

4. Write the area represented by each of your polygons. ______________________________

5. Estimate the area of the island in square kilometers. ______________________________

6. How accurate do you think your estimate is? Explain your answer. ______________________________

   ____

Extend It

Do you think you could accurately estimate the length of the island's shoreline by finding the sum of the outside edges of the polygons you drew? On a separate sheet of paper, explain your answer.

Teacher Notes

Extend: Estimate Area

Objective Use formulas for the area of a rectangle and the area of a triangle to estimate the area of an island shown on a map.
Materials centimeter ruler

Using the Extend (Activities to use after Lesson 3)

Relatively few map features are perfect polygons. However, an approximation of the areas of a map's features can be calculated by superimposing triangles and rectangles over the features and then finding the areas of the polygons. In this activity, students use the formulas for the area of a rectangle and the area of a triangle to estimate the area of an island shown on a map. The Extend It encourages students to consider the accuracy of their estimates.

Math Journal You may wish to have students use their *Math Journals* to answer the Extend It question.

Going Beyond Have students use an atlas to find maps of other islands. Have them superimpose triangles and rectangles on a copy of the map to estimate each island's area.

Solutions

1. *Answers may vary. Sample:*

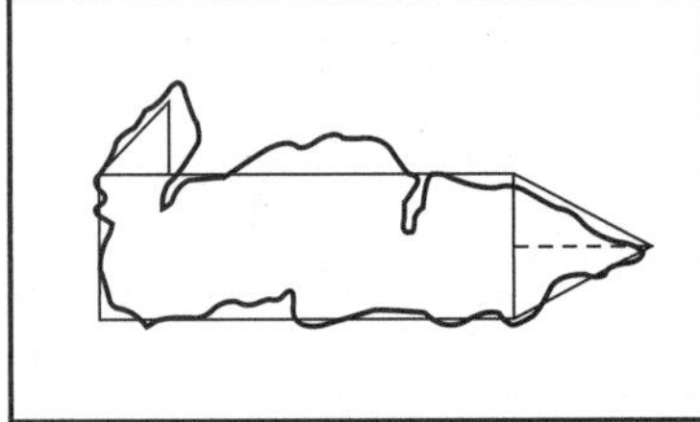

2. *Answers may vary. Sample:* triangle: 0.5 cm^2; rectangle: 12 cm^2; triangle: 1 cm^2; triangle: 1 cm^2
3. 100 km^2
4. *Answers may vary. Sample:* triangle: 50 km^2; rectangle: 1,200 km^2; triangle: 100 km^2; triangle: 100 km^2
5. *Estimates may vary, but should be close to 1,450 km^2.*
6. *Answers may vary. Sample:* I think my estimate is fairly accurate because the polygons I drew cover most of the island.

Extend It *Answers may vary. Sample:* No, because the shoreline is not straight. The different bays and inlets shown indicate that the shoreline would be longer than the perimeter of the polygons drawn.

Name ______________________ Date __________

Planetary Circumferences

Imagine that Earth could be split in half at the equator. The distance around the equator would resemble a circle with a diameter of 7,920 miles! You could use this diameter and the formula for the circumference of a circle to find the Earth's *equatorial circumference*. The equatorial circumference is the distance around Earth at the equator.

1. Use a calculator to calculate the Earth's equatorial circumference to the nearest mile. Use 3.14 for π. __________

Use a calculator to complete the table below. Round each number to the nearest mile.

	Planet	Diameter (in miles)	Equatorial Circumference (in miles)
2.	Mercury	3,032	
3.	Venus	7,522	
4.	Mars		13,232
5.	Jupiter		272,866

6. **Create** On a separate sheet of paper, write diameters for 5 imaginary planets. Be sure to give your planets names. One of your planets should have a diameter greater than any diameter shown in the table above. One of your planets should have a lesser diameter than any shown above. Calculate the equatorial circumference of each planet to the nearest mile and display the results in a table.

Connect It

Do you think Earth's equator is a perfect circle? On a separate sheet of paper, explain why or why not.

Teacher Notes

Connect: Planetary Circumferences

Objective Apply the formula for the circumference of a circle to find the equatorial circumference of planets in the solar system.
Materials calculator

Using the Connect (Activities to use after Lesson 5)

Students are most likely familiar with the concept of the equator. They may not be aware that the other planets in the solar system have equators as well. In this activity, students use the mean diameters of the planets to calculate each planet's circumference. The Connect It guides students to think about the implications of a variation in the calculated and measured values of Earth's equatorial circumference.

Math Journal You may wish to have students use their *Math Journals* to answer Exercise 6 and the Connect It question.

Going Beyond Have students research the lengths of planetary days. Then have them divide each planet's circumference by the length of its day to find the speed of rotation at the planet's equator. Have students compare the planets' rotational speeds.

Solutions

1. 24,869
2. 9,520
3. 23,619
4. 4,214
5. 86,900
6. *Answers may vary. Sample:*

Planet	Diameter (in miles)	Equatorial Circumference (in miles)
Aster	963	3,024
Bluebell	2,741	8,607
Marva	10,512	33,008
Neon	58,004	182,133
Triton	111,764	350,939

Connect It *Answers may vary. Sample:* No, because the Earth's surface is not smooth. Some landforms found along the equator are at higher elevations than other landforms.

Name ______________________ Date ____________

Triangular Pyramids

Round objects like oranges can be stacked in the shape of a triangular pyramid.

Look at the oranges stacked below.

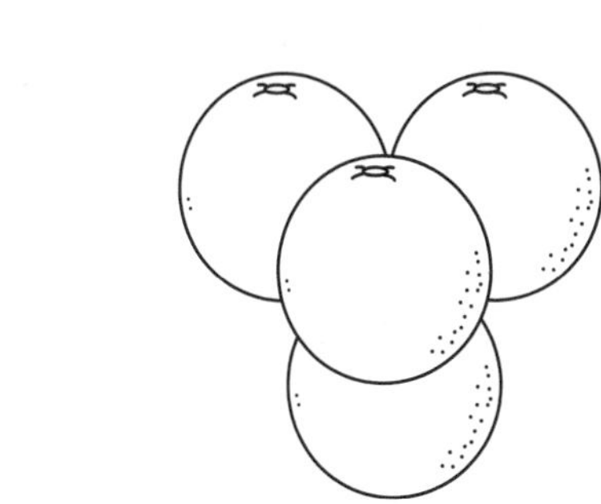 • 2 layers • 2 oranges along each side of the base	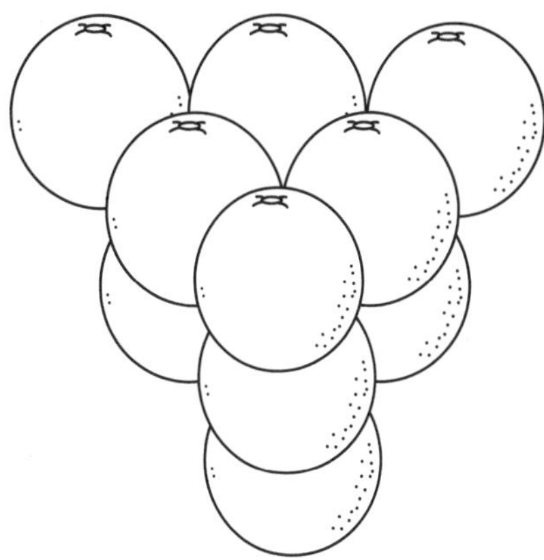 • 3 layers • 3 oranges along each side of the base

1. How many oranges would there be in the base of a pyramid with 4 layers? ________

   How many oranges would there be along each side of the base? ________

2. How many oranges would there be in the base of a pyramid with 5 layers? ________

   How many oranges would there be along each side of the base? ________

3. How many more oranges would there be in the base of the 5-layer pyramid than the 4-layer pyramid? ________

4. **Create** Write a rule to tell how many oranges there will be along each side of the base of a triangular pyramid with *x* layers. ________

   ____

Explore It

Could you make stacks of oranges in the shape of a rectangular prism or cylinder? On a separate sheet of paper, explain.

Teacher Notes

Explore: Triangular Pyramids

Objective Use stacks of oranges to explore the shape of a triangular pyramid.

Using the Explore (Activities to use after Lesson 1)

This activity leads students to understand how the properties of a triangular pyramid (i.e., widest at its base) make it an ideal figure for stacking objects such as oranges. Students are guided to see how the number of oranges along each side of the base in a triangular pyramid is related to the number of layers in the pyramid. Students write a rule to generalize this relationship. In the Explore It, students explore whether oranges could be stacked in the shapes of other solid figures.

Math Journal You may wish to have students use their *Math Journals* to answer the Explore It question.

Going Beyond Have students describe how their calculations would be different if the oranges were stacked in the shape of a square pyramid.

Solutions

1. 10 oranges; 4 oranges
2. 15 oranges; 5 oranges
3. 5 more oranges
4. *Answers may vary. Sample:* A triangular pyramid with *x* layers will have *x* oranges along each side of its base.

Explore It *Answers may vary. Sample:* No. You could not. Rectangular prisms and cylinders are not wider at the base than at the top. The oranges would fall over.

Name ______________________ Date __________

Nets

This net can be folded to make a cube.

A.

1. Which of the three nets below can be folded to make the exact same cube? ________

B.

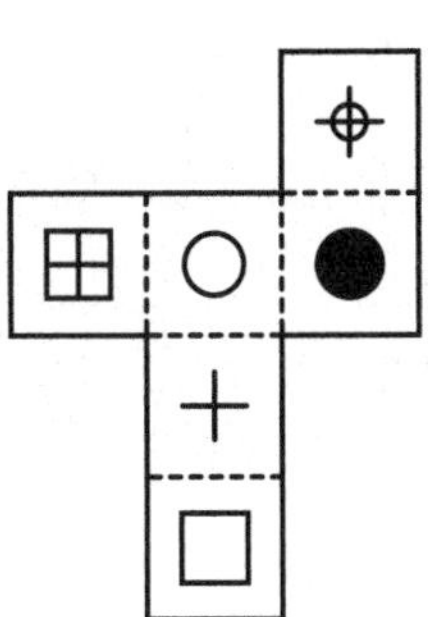

C.

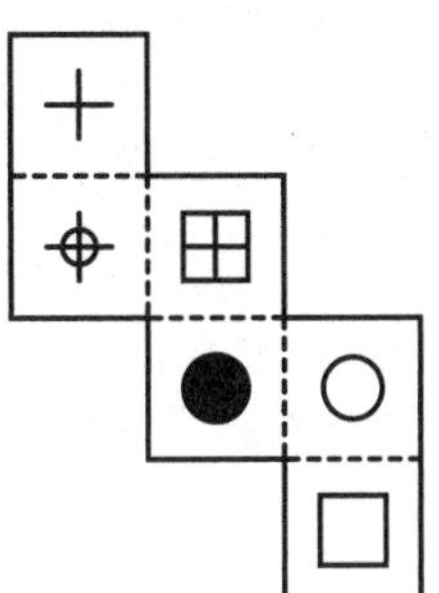

D.

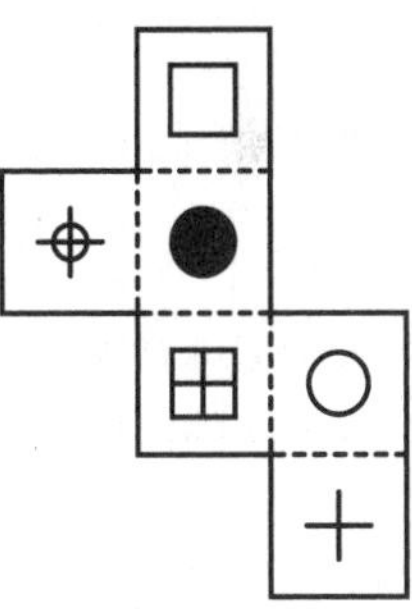

2. **Predict** If you switched the ● and + symbols in net A, then which net could be folded to make the exact same cube? How do you know? ______________________

____

The cubes below were made by folding net B. Draw the missing symbols.

3.

4.

5.

6.

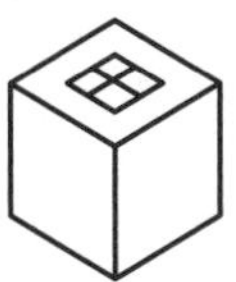

Extend It

How many different ways can you complete the cube with missing symbols in Exercise 6? On a separate sheet of paper, explain how you know.

Teacher Notes

Extend: Nets

Objective Identify nets of different cubes to find identical cubes.

Using the Extend (Activities to use after Lesson 3)

Students have learned about nets for various solid figures. The emphasis has been on which figure each net will make when folded, not on the relative positions of the faces. In this activity, students extend their understanding of nets by using symbols to differentiate the faces on a cube. Students must not only consider what shape each net will make, but also which nets will make cubes with the same arrangement of symbols. Students are then asked to complete the missing symbols on a cube when only three faces of a cube are shown.

Math Journal You may wish to have students use their *Math Journals* to answer the Extend It question.

Going Beyond Have students use a different symbol for each face on a cube. Then have students make 3 different nets for the cube.

Solutions

1. Net D
2. *Answers may vary. Sample:* Net C, because it is the same as net A except two faces are switched. Now that net A has those faces switched, net C makes the same cube as net A.
3. 
4. 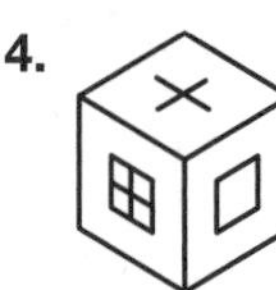
5. 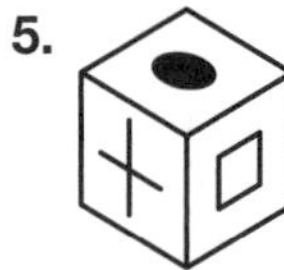
6. *Answers may vary. Samples:*

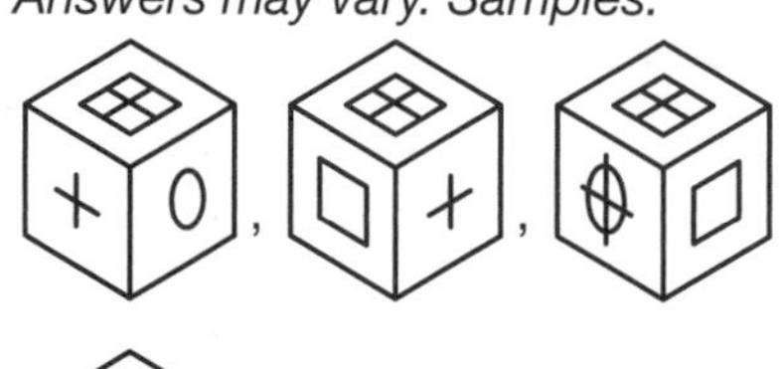

Extend It *Answers may vary. Sample:* There are 4 ways to complete the cube with missing symbols, because the face shown borders 4 other faces.

Name ______________________ Date ____________

Area and Volume

Look at the figures below.

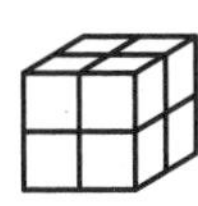

Figure A

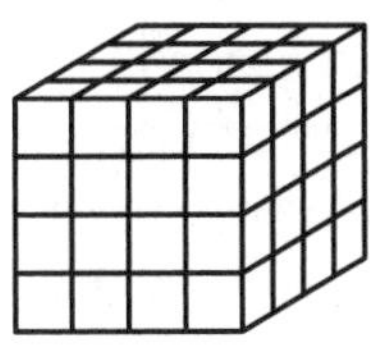

Figure B

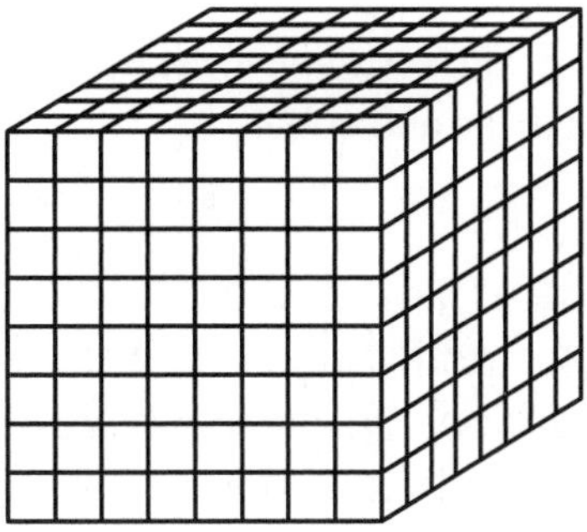

Figure C

Use the figures to complete the table.

	Length of One Side (units)	Area of One Side (square units)	Volume (cubic units)
Figure A			
Figure B			
Figure C			

1. **Create** Write a rule that describes how the area of a square is affected when you double the length of each side.

   ____

2. **Create** Write a rule that describes how the volume of a cube is affected when you double the length of each side.

   ____

Connect It

How does the volume of a solid figure change if only one dimension is multiplied by 2? On a separate sheet of paper, explain your answer.

Teacher Notes

Connect: Area and Volume

Objective Examine the relationship between side length, area, and volume of squares and cubes.

Using the Connect (Activities to use after Lesson 6)

This activity guides students through an examination of the relationship between side lengths, area, and volume of squares and cubes. When you multiply the sides of a square by 2, the area is multiplied by 4. In the case of a cube, when you multiply the side of each square face by 2, the volume is multiplied by 8. These relationships may not be intuitively obvious to students. This activity leads students to make these conclusions on their own. The Connect It encourages students to determine how the volume of a solid figure is affected when you change only one dimension.

Math Journal You may wish to have students use their *Math Journals* to answer the Connect It question.

Going Beyond Have students use their rule to estimate the volume of cubes of varying side lengths.

Solutions

	Length of One Side (units)	Area of One Side (square units)	Volume (cubic units)
Figure A	**2**	**4**	**8**
Figure B	**4**	**16**	**64**
Figure C	**8**	**64**	**512**

1. *Answers may vary. Sample:* When you multiply each side of a square by 2, the area increases by a factor of 4, or 2^2.
2. *Answers may vary. Sample:* When you multiply each side of a cube by 2, the volume increases by a factor of 8, or 2^3.

Connect It *Answers may vary. Sample:* The volume would increase by a factor of 2. For each additional dimension that you multiply by 2, the volume would increase by an additional factor of 2.

Name ______________________ Date __________

Ratios in the Garden

You can use ratios to describe a garden with different types of plants. Look at the plan of the garden at the right. The garden contains flowers, lettuce, and tomatoes.

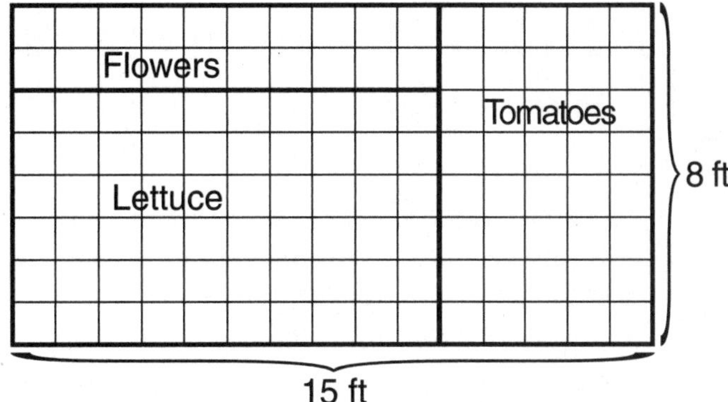

1. What is the ratio of the area of the lettuce to the area of the entire garden?

____

2. What is the ratio of the area of the flowers to the area of the lettuce?

____

3. Suppose the area planted with tomatoes was doubled. What would be the ratio of the area with tomatoes to the area of the entire garden? Explain how you found your answer.

____

____

4. **Create** Now plan a new garden. You want the ratio of lettuce to flowers to tomatoes to be 5:4:3. Use the grid at the right to draw the plan of your garden.

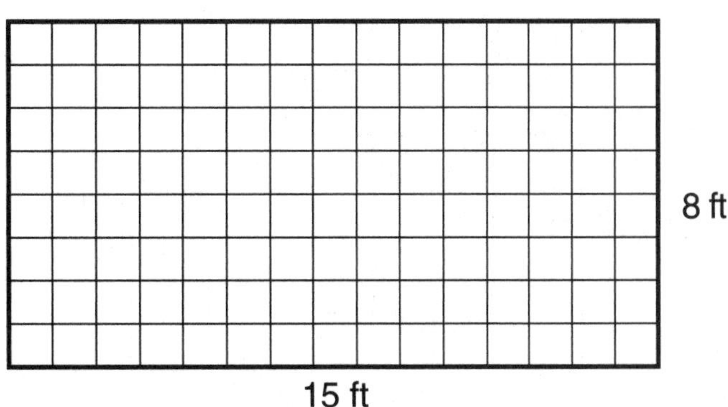

Explore It

Is there only one possible way to draw the garden plan in Exercise 4? On a separate sheet of paper, explain how you know.

Teacher Notes

Explore: Ratios in the Garden

Objective Use a garden plan to write ratios.

Using the Explore (Activities for use after Lesson 1)

In this activity, students use a garden plan along with their knowledge of area to calculate the ratios of the area of different sections of a garden. Students are asked to find a ratio if the area of a section of the garden is doubled. Students then create their own garden plan based on given ratios.

Math Journal You may wish to have students use their *Math Journals* to answer the Explore It question.

Going Beyond Have students create their own garden plan with 4 different types of plants. Have them calculate the ratios of the areas planted with each type of plant.

Solutions

1. 1:2
2. 1:3
3. 2:3; *Answers may vary. Sample:* The area of the tomatoes would double, from 40 square feet to 80 square feet. The ratio of the area of the tomatoes to the area of the entire garden would be 80:120, or 2:3.
4. *Answers may vary. Sample:*

Tomatoes
Flowers
Lettuce

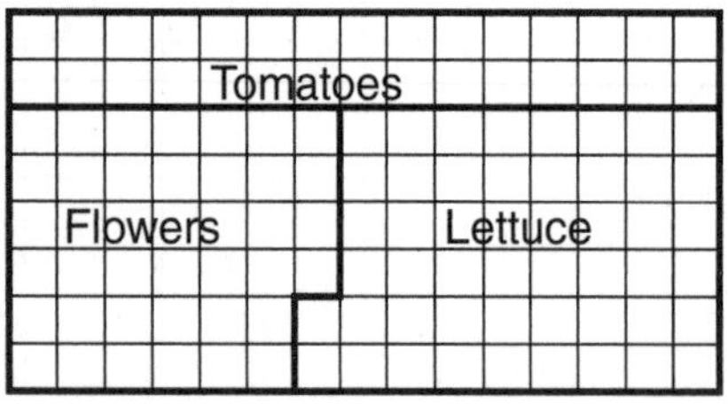

Explore It No. There are many ways to draw the garden plan. The only requirement is that you have 50 square feet planted with lettuce, 40 square feet planted with flowers, and 30 square feet planted with tomatoes.

Name ______________________ Date __________

Rates

A car travels 200 miles at a constant rate in 4 hours. How far will the car travel in 5 hours? You can solve this problem using equivalent ratios.

First, write what you know as a ratio.	Then, find the equivalent ratio.
200 miles in 4 hours $\frac{200}{4}$	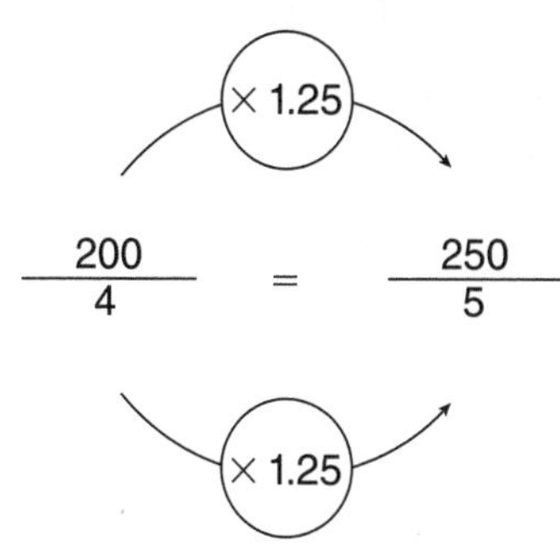 $\frac{200}{4}$ is equivalent to $\frac{250}{5}$

The car travels ______ miles in 5 hours.

1. Use equivalent ratios to find how far the car will travel in 6 hours.

   Explain how you found your answer. ______________________

2. What is the unit rate in miles per hour that the car travels? ______________________

   How can you use the unit rate to find the distance the car travels

   in 6 hours? ______________________

3. **Compare and Contrast** How is using equivalent ratios similar to using unit rates to find distance traveled? How is it different? ______________________

Extend It

Suppose that the ratio of distance *X* to distance *Y* is 7 to 5. Explain how you could find possible values for the amount of time it takes to travel distance *X* and distance *Y*. Is there more than one set of possible values?

Teacher Notes

Extend: Rates

Objective Use equivalent ratios to solve problems with rates.

Using the Extend (Activities for use after Lesson 3)

This activity extends students' understanding of equivalent ratios by using them to find rates. Students will use equivalent ratios to solve rate problems. Critical thinking questions ask students to compare this method to the method of finding unit rates. In the Extend It, students make a generalization based on an abstract rate problem.

Math Journal You may wish to have students use their *Math Journals* to answer the Extend It question.

Going Beyond Have students select other ratios for distance *X* to distance *Y* and find possible values for the amount of time it takes to travel those distances.

Solutions

250

1. 300 miles; Write the equivalent ratios $\frac{200}{4}$ and $\frac{?}{6}$. Multiply the term 4 by 1.5 to get the term 6. So, multiply the term 200 by 1.5 to get the missing term, 300.
2. 50 miles per hour; multiply 50 miles per hour by 6 hours to find a distance of 300 miles.
3. *Answers may vary. Sample:* Similar: In both methods you find equivalent ratios. Different: Using equivalent ratios you multiply to find the missing term. Using a unit rate, you divide to find an equivalent ratio, then multiply that rate by the number of hours.

Extend It If the ratio of distance *X* to distance *Y* is 7:5, then the ratio of the time it takes to travel distance *X* to the time it takes to travel distance *Y* is 7:5. *X* and *Y* can have any value as long as the ratio of *X* to *Y* is 7:5.

Name ____________________ Date __________

Estimating Distances on a Map

Look at the map below. The scale is 1 cm: 0.05 mi.

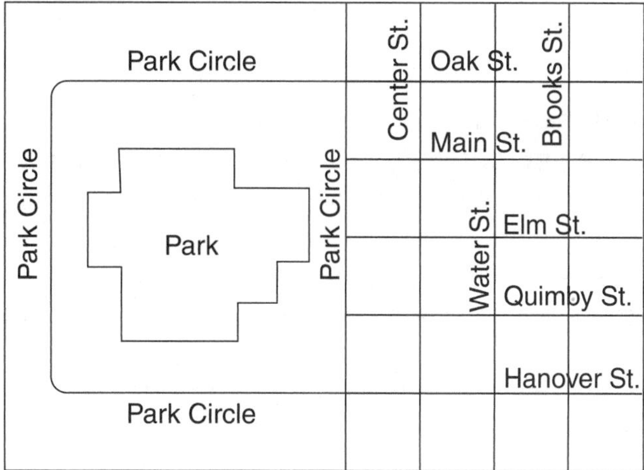

1. If you walk on Center Street, what is the approximate distance from Hanover Street to Oak Street? ____________________

2. If you walk along the streets shown, about how far is it to walk from the corner of Quimby Street and Brooks Street to the corner of Center Street and Oak Street?

   ____

3. **Analyze** If you walk 2 miles per hour, about how long would it take you to walk around the perimeter of the park? ____________________

4. **Explain** What is the shortest route from the corner of Oak Street and Water Street to the corner of Brooks Street and Hanover Street? How do you know?

   ____

Connect It

Suppose you start walking at the corner of Water Street and Oak Street. You walk along Water Street towards Hanover Street at 1 mile per hour. What intersection will you be closest to after 10 minutes of walking? Explain.

Teacher Notes

Connect: Estimating Distances on a Map

Objective Estimate walking times from one location to another using a map.

Using the Connect (Activities for use after Lesson 5)

Students have been introduced to scale drawings, but have not used estimation to decide about how long it takes to walk from one location to another using a map. In the Connect It, they estimate a location based on a starting point, walking rate, and elapsed time. Thus they integrate the concepts of scale and rate of travel.

Math Journal You may wish to have students use their *Math Journals* to answer the Connect It question.

Going Beyond Have students estimate which takes more time: walking 2 miles per hour from the corner of Hanover Street and Brooks Street to the corner of Quimby Street and Center Street, or driving around Park Circle at 10 miles per hour.

Solutions

1. *Answers may vary. Sample:* about 0.2 miles
2. *Answers may vary. Sample:* about 0.25 miles
3. *Answers may vary. Sample:* about 15 minutes
4. *Answers may vary. Sample:* Walk along Oak Street to Brooks Street, then turn and walk along Brooks Street to Hanover Street. It is the shortest distance, but there are several other routes that are exactly the same distance.

Connect It *Answers may vary. Sample:* The corner of Water Street and Quimby Street. Each block is about $\frac{1}{20}$ of a mile, so it takes about 3 minutes to walk each block at 1 mile per hour. After 10 minutes, you have walked about 3 blocks.

Name ______________________ Date ____________

Determining Percents

You can use percents to describe the shaded portion of a figure.

Write the percent of each figure that is shaded.

1. 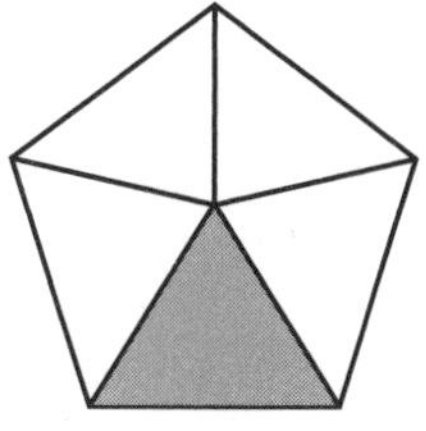 ______

2. 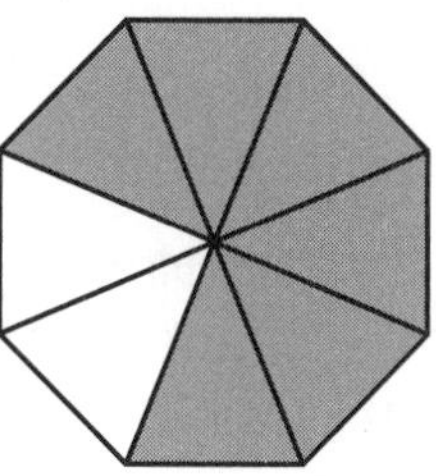 ______

3. 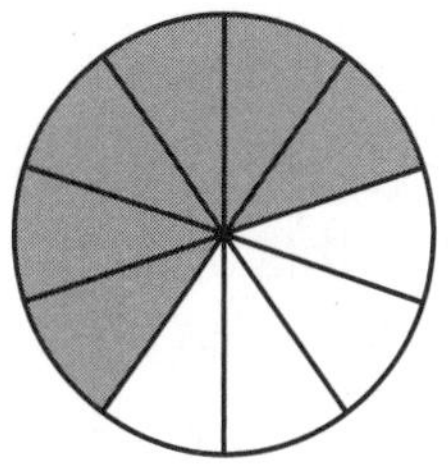 ______

4. 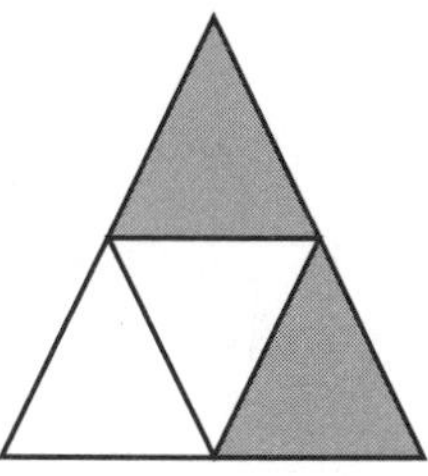 ______

5. 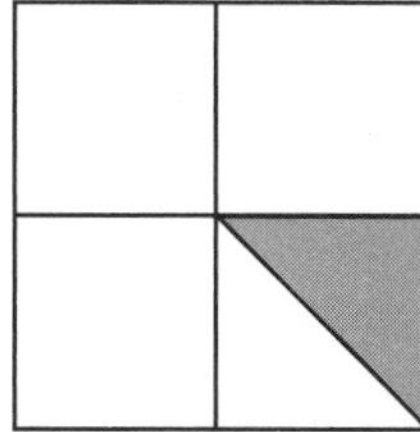 ______

6. 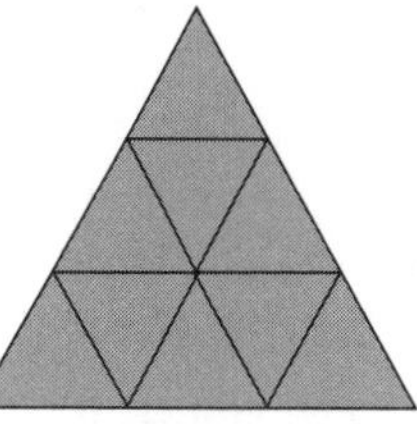 ______

Estimate whether the shaded area of each figure is less than 50%, greater than 50%, or about 50%.

7. 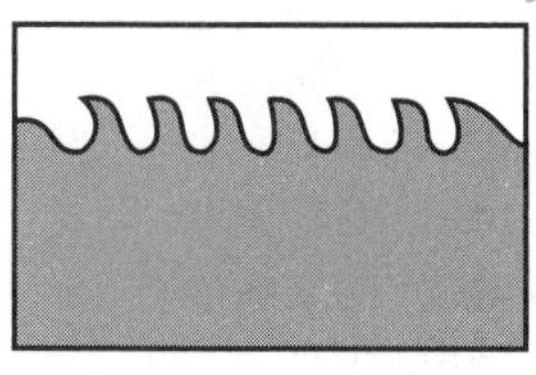 ______

8.  ______

9. 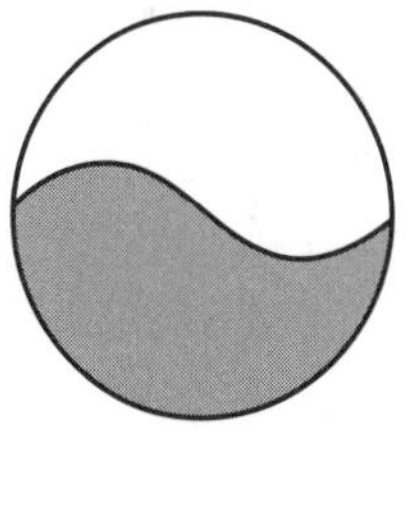 ______

10. **Explain** Is it possible for more than 100% of each figure to be shaded?

    Why or why not? ______________________

Explore It

Can you increase the percent of shading in a figure by more than 100%? Explain your answer.

Teacher Notes

Explore: Determining Percents

Objective Use shaded sections of non-grid figures to explore the concept of percent.

Using the Explore (Activities to use after Lesson 1)

In this activity, students find percents of various shaded figures. Students are asked to assess the shaded percent of irregular shapes as less than 50%, greater than 50%, or about 50%. The critical thinking question and the Explore It encourage students to consider percents greater than 100%.

Math Journal You may wish to have students use their *Math Journals* to answer the Explore It question.

Going Beyond Have students draw their own irregular figures and use estimation to shade different percents of each figure.

Solutions

1. 20%
2. 75%
3. 60%
4. 50%
5. 12.5%
6. 100%
7. greater than 50%
8. less than 50%
9. about 50%
10. *Answers may vary. Sample:* No, because 100% of the figure is the whole figure. You cannot shade any more of the figure.

Explore It *Answers may vary. Sample:* Yes. If a figure has 10 equal sections with 1 shaded section, then 10% of the figure is shaded. If you shade 2 more sections, then you have increased the shaded section of the figure by 200%.

Name ______________________ Date __________

Use Percents

The fictional country of Baronia taxes its citizens on the amount of money they earn. This table shows what percent tax citizens pay on different ranges of their income.

Income Range	Tax Rate
$0–$8,000	10%
$8,001–$25,000	15%
$25,001 and above	20%

- The first $8,000 earned is taxed at 10%.
- Income in the second level, between $8,001 and $25,000, is taxed at 15%.
- Income in the third level, $25,001 and above, is taxed at 20%.

Each income range is taxed at a different rate. You add the tax at each level of income to find the total tax.

For example, Citizen A earns $11,000. How much tax does she pay?

$8,000 × 0.10 = ______ $3,000 × 0.15 = ______

______ + ______ = ______

↑ taxed at 10% ↑ taxed at 15% ↑ total tax

Use a calculator and the table to answer the questions.

1. Citizen B has an income of $21,000. How much tax does Citizen B pay?

Explain how you found your answer. ______________________

____

2. Suppose Citizen B had earned an additional $3,000. How much additional tax would Citizen B pay? ______________________

3. **Analyze** Citizen C's income is taxed at 15%. What is the least tax that Citizen C could pay? ______________ the greatest tax? ______________

Extend It

Suppose Citizen A's income is tripled. Calculate the tax that Citizen A now pays. Explain your answer.

Teacher Notes

Extend: Use Percents

Objective Use percents of number to find fictional income tax on earnings.
Materials calculator

Using the Extend (Activities to use after Lesson 3)

In this activity, students use a fictional income table and graduated tax rates to find tax paid by fictional citizens. Students are led through a guided example that shows how to calculate the percent of tax for each income level. Students then find the total tax by finding the sum of the taxes at each income level. Students use the table to answer additional questions. In the Extend It students use percents to find the total tax paid at a greater income level.

Math Journal You may wish to have students use their *Math Journals* to answer the Extend It question.

Going Beyond Ask students if two citizens with $30,000 and $40,000 incomes, respectively, pay the same amount of tax on the first $25,000 of their income. Students should realize that the tax paid on the first $25,000 is the same for both citizens.

Solutions

$800; $450; $800 + $450 = $1,250

1. $2,750. *Answers may vary. Sample:* The first $8,000 is taxed at 10%. $8,000 × 0.10 = $800. Find the difference between the income earned, $21,000, and the first $8,000 earned. $21,000 − $8,000 = $13,000. This is taxed at 15%. $13,000 × 0.15 = $1,950. Add $800 and $1,950. $800 + $1,950 = $2,750.
2. $450
3. $800.15; $3,350.

Extend It *Answers may vary. Sample:* Citizen A's income is now $33,000. The first $8,000 earned is taxed at 10%. $8,000 × 0.10 = $800. Find the difference between the income earned, $33,000, and the first $8,000 earned. $33,000 − $8,000 = $25,000. This is taxed at 15%. $25,000 × 0.15 = $3,750 Add: $800 + $3,750 = $4,550

Name ______________________ Date __________

People Percentages

Demographics are statistics that describe human populations. Some demographics use percents to give information about the people that they describe.

These tables describe the people who live in Galveston County, Texas. The total population of the county is about 250,000 people.

Age	Percent
Under 5 years	7%
5–18 years	20%
18–65 years	62%
Over 65 years	11%

Gender	Percent
Female	51%
Male	49%

Use the tables and a calculator to answer the questions.

1. About how many people in Galveston County are female? ______________________

2. Which age group contains the greatest number of people? ______________________

   the least number? ______________________

3. About how many people are in each of the age groups described in Question 2?

   ____

4. There are about 50,000 members of one age group in Galveston County.

   Which age group is it? ______________________

5. Estimate the number of people in Galveston County who are female and the number who are male. Explain how you found your estimates. ______________________

   ____

   ____

Connect It

Can you use the percent of females in Galveston County to find the number of females who are between 18 and 65 years old? Explain your answer.

Teacher Notes

Connect: People Percentages

Objective Find the percent of numbers to analyze demographic information.
Materials calculator

Using the Connect (Activities to use after Lesson 5)

Demographic information is often provided using percents. In this activity, students analyze demographic tables representing information about Galveston County, Texas. Students use their knowledge of percents to interpret and analyze the data to solve problems. The Connect It encourages students to consider some of the potential limitations of demographic information.

Math Journal You may wish to have students use their *Math Journals* to answer the Connect It question.

Going Beyond Have students research other types of demographic information. Have them write word problems about the data that use percents.

Solutions

1. about 127,500 people
2. 18–65 years; under 5 years
3. 18–65 years: about 155,000 people; under 5 years: about 17,500 people
4. 5–18 years
5. *Answers may vary. Sample:* There are about 125,000 people who are female, and 125,000 people who are male. The population is 51% female and 49% male. This is about 50% female and 50% male. I divided the total population of 250,000 by 2 to get 125,000.

Connect It *Answers may vary. Sample:* No, because the percent of females in the entire county is not necessarily the same as the percent of females in each individual age group.

Name ______________________ Date __________

Combinations

Combinations are often used on locks. Some locks have more possible combinations than others.

Calculate the total number of possible combinations for each of these locks.

Each number wheel contains the digits 0–9.

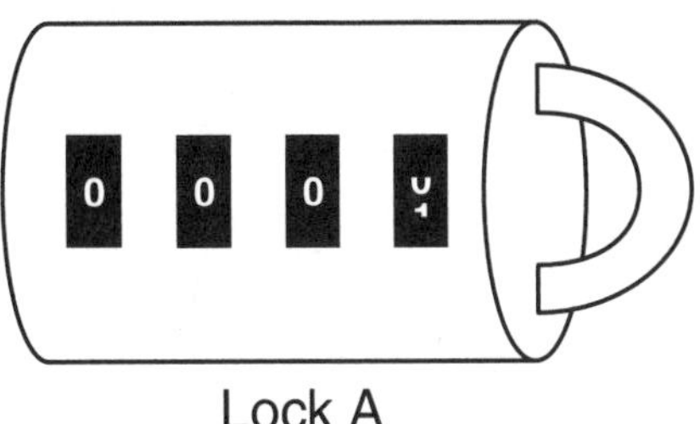

Lock A

Possible combinations: __________

This lock contains the numbers 1–30. The combination is made by turning the dial to three numbers, as in 4-21-17.

Possible combinations:

____

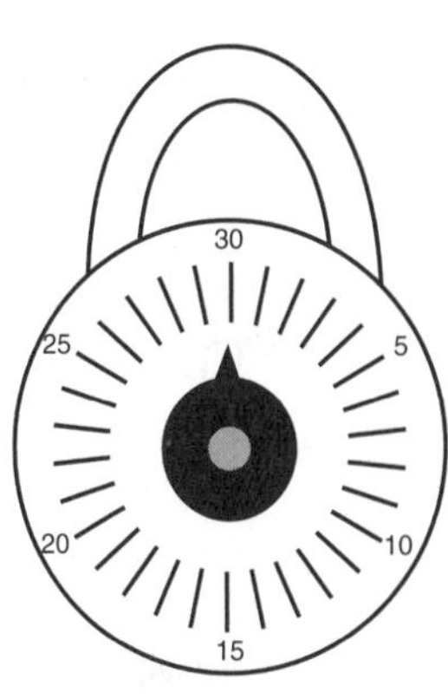

Lock B

1. Which lock has more possible combinations? __________
2. **Analyze** Which lock would you use to lock up your bicycle? Why? __________
3. Write an expression to calculate the number of different possible combinations of four numbers from 0–9. __________
4. Write an expression to calculate the number of different possible combinations of three numbers from 1–30. __________
5. **Generalize** Write a rule for calculating the total number of different possible combinations of numbers. __________

Explore It

Every telephone number in the United States is a unique 10-digit number (3-digit area code + 3-digit exchange + 4-digit number). Telephone numbers cannot begin with 0, 1, 411-, or 911-. How many possible telephone numbers could there be in the United States, using the digits 0–9? How many could there be if numbers could begin with 0; 1; 411; or 911? Explain your answer.

Teacher Notes

Explore: Combinations

Objective Explore the possible combinations of different locks.

Using the Explore (Activities to use after Lesson 1)

In this activity, students explore combinations with different numbers of elements and different numbers of choices for each element. Students see how these variables affect the number of possible combinations. The exercises on this page present combinations in real-life, simple contexts. Critical thinking questions encourage students to apply their knowledge to write expressions and rules. The Explore It asks students to apply their understanding to a new situation.

Math Journal You may wish to have students use their *Math Journals* to answer the Explore It.

Going Beyond Have students complete the Explore It activity for telephone numbers in another country. Provide guidance for using a resource to learn about international telephone codes and telephone number formats in other countries. Explain that there is no real way to determine the exact number of telephone numbers in either the United States or the world because numbers are constantly being added or removed from service.

Solutions

10,000; 27,000

1. Lock B
2. *Answers may vary. Sample:* I would rather use Lock B, because there are more possible combinations, so it would be more difficult for someone to guess my combination. *Or* I would rather use Lock A because if I forgot part of my combination, I wouldn't have to try as many combinations until I found the right one.
3. $10 \times 10 \times 10 \times 10$ or 10^4
4. $30 \times 30 \times 30$ or 30^3
5. *Answers may vary. Sample:* To calculate the total number of possible combinations, raise the number of choices per digit to the power equal to the number of digits.

Explore It Possible phone numbers without 0, 1, 411, or 911: There are 1,000,000,000 numbers beginning with 0; 1,000,000,000 numbers beginning with 1; 10,000,000 numbers beginning with 411; and 10,000,000 numbers beginning with 911. Subtract all those prohibited numbers from 10,000,000,000. The answer is 7,980,000,000.

Possible phone numbers with 0, 1, 411, or 911: All numbers 0000000000–9999999999 are possible phone numbers. That means there are 10,000,000,000 possible phone numbers.

Name ______________________ Date __________

Probability at Play

In this game, you toss rings onto colored pegs. Each time you toss a ring, it will land on one of the pegs. The probability that a ring will land on a peg is 1. The chart below shows the number of pegs of each color. Calculate the probability of a ring landing on each color. Express each probability as a fraction in simplest form.

Peg Color	White	Pink	Red	Orange	Yellow	Green	Blue	Purple	Black
Number of Pegs	30	50	2	14	10	20	4	40	30
Probability for One Ring									

1. Mark the probability you found for each color on the "probability line" below. You can use a common denominator to make it easier to plot each probability.

Impossible — Equally Likely — Certain

Less Likely ← - - - - - - - - - - - - - - - -   - - - - - - - - - - - - - - - - → *More Likely*

0 ———————————————————————— 1

2. **Hypothesize** Suppose you were in charge of this game at a carnival. You have 9 prizes valued from $1 to $9. Each peg color has a different prize. How would you decide which color gets the $1 prize? the $9 prize?

   Explain your answer. ______________________

   ____

   ____

3. **Analyze** If you could pick a color and then win a prize if another player's ring landed on that color, which color would you pick? Why? ______________________

   ____

Extend It

How could you change the ring toss game to make it more likely that someone will get the $9 prize? less likely? Explain your answer.

Teacher Notes

Extend: Probability at Play

Objective Calculate and compare relative probabilities of different outcomes.

Using the Extend (Activities to use after Lesson 3)
In this activity, students explore theoretical probability as it relates to games. Students are provided with an opportunity to see the advantage that understanding probability provides when making choices. Critical thinking questions encourage students to use their understanding of probabilities to make choices. Students also have an opportunity to practice writing fractions in simplest form. The Extend It challenges students to change the game in a way that makes certain probabilities more likely and less likely.

Math Journal You may wish to have students use their *Math Journals* to answer the Extend It.

Going Beyond Have students list factors that might cause experimental data for the ring toss game to differ from the theoretical probability that they calculated. Possible answers include: Pegs of a certain color may be located farther away. Also, people generally aim at the pegs with the higher value prizes, which could increase the probability of a ring landing on that color.

Solutions

White	Pink	Red	Orange	Yellow	Green	Blue	Purple	Black
$\frac{3}{20}$	$\frac{1}{4}$	$\frac{1}{100}$	$\frac{7}{100}$	$\frac{1}{20}$	$\frac{1}{10}$	$\frac{1}{50}$	$\frac{1}{5}$	$\frac{3}{20}$

1.

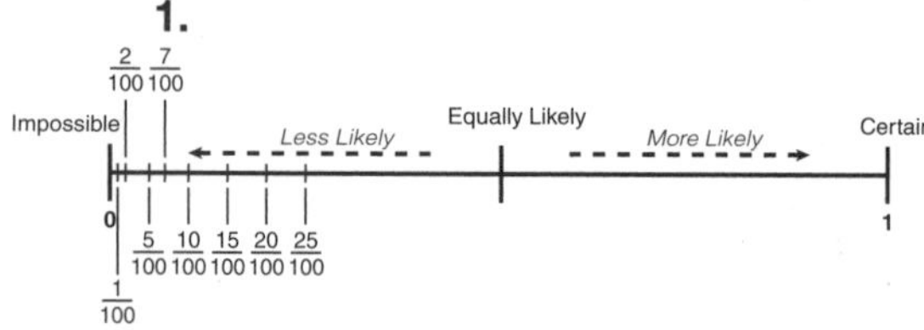

2. *Answers may vary. Sample:* I'd give the $9 prize for red, since it's the least likely outcome; I'd give the $1 prize for pink, since it's the most likely outcome; I'd give the remaining prizes (in order of value from least to greatest) for blue, yellow, orange, green, black/white, and purple.

3. *Answers may vary. Sample:* I would pick pink because this would give the best chance of winning a prize.

Extend It *Answers may vary. Sample:* You could make it more likely that someone would get the $9 prize by increasing the number of pegs that had the $9 prize. You could make it less likely that someone would get the $9 prize by decreasing the number of pegs that had the $9 prize. You could also add more pegs of different colors that had prizes of a lower value.

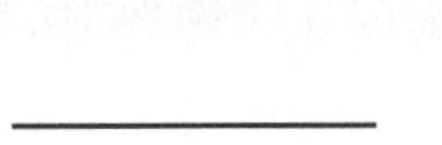

Name ______________________________ Date ____________

The Weather

This chart shows the number of tornadoes in the United States during each month for 5 years.

	Jan	Feb	Mar	Apr	May	Jun	Jul	Aug	Sep	Oct	Nov	Dec
2002	3	2	45	116	204	97	68	86	60	55	95	21
2001	5	30	33	135	241	248	120	69	84	116	110	22
2000	16	56	103	136	241	135	148	52	47	63	48	26
1999	212	22	56	177	310	289	102	79	56	17	7	15
1998	47	72	72	82	310	376	82	61	104	86	26	6
Average												

1. Find the 5-year average for each month. Round each average to the nearest whole number.

2. Use the averages you found to determine the probability that a tornado will occur in each month.

   a. Jan ____________ **b.** Feb ____________ **c.** Mar ____________

   d. Apr ____________ **e.** May ____________ **f.** Jun ____________

   g. Jul ____________ **h.** Aug ____________ **i.** Sep ____________

   j. Oct ____________ **k.** Nov ____________ **l.** Dec ____________

3. **Generalize** During which month do the most tornadoes occur? ________________________

   the fewest? ________________________

4. **Predict** What is the probability that a tornado occurs

   a. next month? ____________ **b.** in August? ____________

   c. from March–May? ____________ **d.** from June–August? ____________

Connect It

Is this method of predicting tornadoes accurate? Explain your answer. What other information might make predictions more accurate?

Teacher Notes

Connect: The Weather

Objective Compare theoretical probability to experimental probability by using past weather information to predict future weather patterns.

Using the Connect (Activities to use after Lesson 5)
In this activity, students explore using experimental probability (past weather data) to extrapolate theoretical probability (weather predictions). Students examine the differences between experimental and theoretical probability. Students also find averages and use rounding in their calculations. Critical thinking questions encourage students to use experimental probabilities to make predictions. The Connect It challenges students to evaluate the quality of this method of making predictions.

Math Journal You may wish to have students use their *Math Journals* to answer the Connect It questions.

Going Beyond Have students use the Internet or other resource to gather data to repeat this activity for other weather phenomena, such as hurricanes or blizzards. Challenge students to find out what other variables are considered by meteorologists when they are predicting tornadoes, such as location, air temperature, humidity, barometric pressure, and so on.

Solutions

1.

Jan	Feb	Mar	Apr	May	Jun	Jul	Aug	Sep	Oct	Nov	Dec
57	36	62	129	261	229	104	69	70	67	57	18

2. **a.** Jan: 0.05; $\frac{5}{100} = \frac{1}{20}$;
b. Feb: 0.03 = $\frac{3}{100}$;
c. Mar: 0.05 = $\frac{5}{100} = \frac{1}{20}$;
d. Apr: 0.11 = $\frac{11}{100}$;
e. May: 0.23 = $\frac{23}{100}$;
f. Jun: 0.20 = $\frac{20}{100} = \frac{1}{5}$;
g. Jul: 0.09 = $\frac{9}{100}$;
h. Aug: 0.06 = $\frac{6}{100} = \frac{3}{50}$;
i. Sep: 0.06 = $\frac{6}{100} = \frac{3}{50}$;
j. Oct: 0.06 = $\frac{6}{100} = \frac{3}{50}$;
k. Nov: 0.05 = $\frac{5}{100} = \frac{1}{20}$;
l. Dec: 0.02 = $\frac{2}{100} = \frac{1}{50}$

3. May; December

4. **a.** *Answers may vary depending on the current month;*
b. $\frac{69}{1,159}$ or $\frac{3}{50}$; **c.** $\frac{452}{1,159}$ or $\frac{39}{100}$;
d. $\frac{402}{1,159}$ or $\frac{7}{20}$

Connect It *See Additional Answers on Page 139.*

Name ________________________ Date ____________

Equations as Clues

You can use what you know about balancing equations to find the values of variables. In the equations below, all of the values are positive whole numbers, and each variable represents the same value. Look at the equations for clues to help you find the values of *r* and *t*.

Write either a whole number or an operation sign (+, −, ×, ÷) in each circle.

a. $r + \bigcirc = 12$

b. $10 = t \bigcirc 5$

c. $400 \div r = \bigcirc$

d. $5 \bigcirc r = 15$

e. $2t - r = \bigcirc$

f. $r \times t = \bigcirc$

g. $(t + 5) \div 4 = \bigcirc$

h. $2t \bigcirc r = 3$

i. $\bigcirc \times r = 30$

1. What are the values of *r* and *t*? ____________

2. Explain Which equations did you solve first to find the values or *r* and *t*?

Explain. ____

____

3. Describe How did you use the information in one equation to find the missing values and operations in another equation? ____________

____

____

4. Give an example of how you used what you know about balancing equations to find the missing value in an equation. ____________

5. Generalize Is it helpful to know that *r* and *t* are whole numbers? Explain.

____

Explore It

On a separate sheet of paper, write a set of equations similar to those above. Write at least five equations and provide answers.

Teacher Notes

Explore: Equations as Clues

Objective Use logic, reasoning, and knowledge of balancing equations to find missing values and operations.

Using the Explore (Activities to use after Lesson 2)

In this activity, students must solve equations related by their common unknown values. Equations become solvable only as the value of missing elements are deduced. A critical thinking question asks students to explain their strategies. In the Explore It, students create their own set of equations with missing values and operations.

Math Journal You may wish to have students use their *Math Journals* to answer the Explore It question.

Going Beyond Have students create a set of related equations using three unknown values.

Solutions

a. $r + \mathbf{2} = 12$ **b.** $10 = t - 5$

c. $400 \div r = \mathbf{\mathit{40}}$ **d.** $5 + r = 15$

e. $2t - r = \mathbf{\mathit{20}}$ **f.** $r \times t = \mathbf{\mathit{150}}$

g. $(t + 5) \div 4 = \mathbf{5}$ **h.** $2t \div r = 3$

i. $\mathbf{3} \times r = 30$

1. $r = 10$, $t = 15$

2. *Answers may vary. Sample:* For *t*, I first solved equations *c* and *d*. Equation *d* narrowed the value of *r* down to 10 or 3. Equation *c* narrowed the value of *r* to 10. For *t*, I started with equations *b* and *g*.

3. *Answers may vary. Sample:* First, I narrowed down to a choice of possible values for the variables. Then, I tested those values in other equations.

4. *Answers may vary. Sample:* Once I discovered that $r = 10$, I was able to substitute 10 into equation *a*. Then I solved and found the missing value, 2.

5. *Answers may vary. Sample:* It is very helpful. If the unknown values did not have to be whole numbers, they could have been many different fractions and decimals.

Explore It *Answers may vary. Check students' work.*

Name ______________________ Date __________

Price Reductions and Increased Sales

The president of You Buy It estimates that his company can sell 8,500 units next year at full price. The accountant thinks that sales will increase by 85 units, or 1% of the original estimate, each time they reduce the price of a unit by 1%.

1. How many units are likely to be sold if the price is not reduced at all?

   Explain. ______________________

2. How many units are likely to be sold if the price is reduced by 1%? How do you know?

   ____

3. **Explain** Does the number of units the company expects to sell increase by the same amount each time the price is reduced by 1%? Why or why not? ______________________

4. Write an equation that describes how many units are likely to be sold for a given number of times that the price is reduced. Let *r* represent the number of price reductions and *s* represent the total number of units likely to be sold.

   ____

5. Use your equation to complete the function table.

r	*s*
0	
1	
2	
3	
4	
5	
10	
20	

Extend It

Is the ratio of consecutive *s* values in the table always the same? On a separate sheet of paper, explain.

Teacher Notes

Extend: Price Reductions and Increased Sales

Objective Explore sales levels as a function of price.

Using the Extend (Activities to use after Lesson 4)

In a supply and demand economy, prices depend on numerous factors. One of these factors is the discounting of prices from their typical level. In this activity, students are guided toward formulating an algebraic function linking discounts and levels of unit sales. Students then calculate values to complete a function table. Critical thinking questions have students examine the table data in different ways. The Extend It asks students to consider the relationship between different values in the table.

Math Journal You may wish to have students use their *Math Journals* to answer the Extend It question.

Going Beyond Have students make a new function table assuming that sales will increase by a percent greater than 1% each time the price is reduced.

Solutions

1. 8,500 units; *Answers may vary. Sample:* The price is not discounted at all, so only 8,500 units are likely to be sold.
2. 8,585 units; *Answers may vary. Sample:* You know they are likely to sell the original 8,500 units plus an additional 85 units because of the 1% reduction in price. 8,500 + 85 = 8,585.
3. *Answers may vary. Sample:* Yes, because each time the price is reduced by 1%, the number of units sold is likely to increase by 85.
4. $s = 8{,}500 + (85 \times r)$
5.

r	*s*
0	8,500
1	8,585
2	8,670
3	8,755
4	8,840
5	8,925
10	9,350
20	10,200

Extend It *Answers may vary. Sample:* No. Each time the price is reduced, the number of units sold increases by 85, but 85 does not represent the same percent of each *s* value. For example, $\frac{8{,}585}{8{,}500}$ does not equal $\frac{8{,}670}{8{,}585}$.

Name ______________________ Date __________

The Cost of a Music CD

The table to the right shows an estimate of where your money might go when you buy a music CD that costs $16.98.

Distribution of Cost of a $16.98 Music CD	
Retail Markup	$6.23
Record Company	$3.93
Advertising, Marketing, Promotion	$3.00
Music Production	$1.08
Royalty to Artist and Songwriter	$1.99
Manufacturing of CD and Album	$0.75
Total Retail Price	**$16.98**

1. To the nearest tenth of a percent, what percent of the total retail price is the manufacturing cost?

____

2. What is the ratio of Advertising, Marketing, and Promotion cost to Manufacturing of CD and Album cost?

____

3. **Decide** Suppose that this ratio decreases by half. What would be the cost for those two categories if the total price remained the same? Explain how you found your answer.

____

4. Write an equation that represents the relationship between the Royalty to Artist and Songwriter, *y*, and the number of CDs sold, *x*. Explain how to solve your equation to find the royalties the artist and songwriter will receive for a given number of CDs sold.

____

5. Suppose the royalties received by an artist and songwriter are $1,293.50. Use your equation to find how many CDs were sold.

____

Connect It

On a separate sheet of paper, show how you could use percents instead of equations to find the royalties for a given number of CDs.

Teacher Notes

Connect: The Cost of a Music CD

Objective Understand tables with related data.

Using the Connect (Activities to use after Lesson 5)

Students have learned the concept of the algebraic function, where the value of one variable is dependent on the value of another variable. In this activity, students see that data must be carefully assessed for the presence of dependent variables, and to determine how those variables are related. Critical thinking questions lead students to consider fixed and variable costs. The Connect It has students explain an alternative method to solving a given problem.

Math Journal You may wish to have students use their *Math Journals* to answer the Connect It question.

Going Beyond Review Exercise 4 with students. Then have students write equations to represent other relationships in the table.

Solutions

1. 4.4%
2. 4:1
3. Advertising, Marketing, and Promotion: $2.50; Manufacturing of CD and Album: $1.25. *Answers may vary. Sample:* The ratio was 4:1. Half of that ratio is 2:1. 2:1 represents 3 parts. The total cost of both categories is $3.75. I divided $3.75 by 3, which is $1.25. 2 of those parts equals $2.50. 1 part equals $1.25.
4. $y = x \times \$1.99$. *Answers may vary. Sample:* You can solve this equation by substituting the number of CDs sold. For example, when 2 CDs are sold, $x = 2$. Substitute 2 in the equation.
   $y = 2 \times \$1.99$
   $y = \$3.98$
5. $\$1,293.50 = x \times \$1.99$
   $\$1,293.50 \div \$1.99 = x$
   $650 = x$
   650 CDs were sold.

Connect It *Answers may vary. Sample:* I would find what percent of the total price of a CD the royalties represent. Rounding to the nearest hundredth, $1.99 \div 16.98 = 0.12$, or 12%. Then I would multiply the number of CDs sold by $16.98 to find the total sales. If 100 CDs were sold, then this would be $1,698.00. Finally, I would multiply the total sales by 12% to find the amount the royalties represent. For 100 CDs sold, this would be $0.12 \times \$1,698.00$, or $203.76.

Name ______________________ Date ____________

Integers and the Motion of a Spring

Suppose you attach a weight to the end of a spring. When you release the weight, it falls and stretches the spring. Next, the spring contracts and the weight rises. Then the weight falls again. This continues until the weight comes to rest. The diagrams below show how far the weight falls and rises.

A. 1st fall	**B.** 1st rise	**C.** 2nd fall	**D.** 2nd rise	**E.** 3rd fall
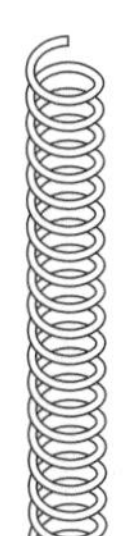		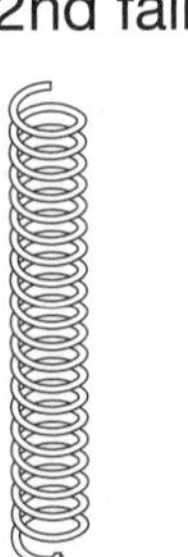		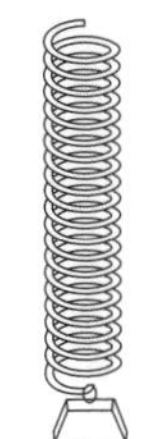
The weight travels a distance of $^{-}6$ cm	The weight travels a distance of $^{+}5$ cm	The weight travels a distance of $^{-}4$ cm	The weight travels a distance of $^{+}3$ cm	The weight travels a distance of $^{-}2$ cm

1. **Create** On a separate sheet of paper, use the information in diagrams A–E above to make a number line. On your number line, plot points that represent the location of the weight in each diagram.

2. Compared to the starting point, at what distance is the weight after the third fall?

   How do you know? ______________________

   ____

3. **Explain** Compared to its location after the first fall, how far has the weight moved after the third fall? How do you know? ______________________

   ____

Explore It

Suppose the weight rises 1 cm on the third rise. On a separate sheet of paper, explain how you can use your number line to find the location of the weight.

Teacher Notes

Explore: Integers and the Motion of a Spring

Objective Use the motion of a weighted spring to investigate integers.

Using the Explore (Activities to use after Lesson 2)

This activity uses the example of a weighted spring moving up and down to investigate integers. Students are given the distance a weighted spring travels as it rises and falls after being released. They must use integers to examine the relative positions of the weight at different points. Students also create their own number line to help them answer the critical thinking questions and the Explore It.

Math Journal You may wish to have students use their *Math Journals* for the Explore It.

Going Beyond Have students use their number line to estimate where the weight will be after a fourth fall.

Solutions

1. A C E D B (points at $^{-}6$, $^{-}5$, $^{-}4$, $^{-}2$, $^{-}1$)

$^{-}7$ $^{-}6$ $^{-}5$ $^{-}4$ $^{-}3$ $^{-}2$ $^{-}1$ 0 $^{+}1$ $^{+}2$ $^{+}3$ $^{+}4$ $^{+}5$ $^{+}6$ $^{+}7$

2. $^{-}4$ cm. *Answers may vary. Sample:* I compared the starting point, 0, to the distance after the third fall, $^{-}4$ cm. The weight moved $^{-}4$ cm.

3. $^{+}2$ cm. *Answers may vary. Sample:* I compared the distance of the weight after the first fall, $^{-}6$ cm, to the distance after the third fall, $^{-}4$ cm. The weight moved $^{+}2$ cm.

Explore It *Answers may vary. Sample:* I find the location of the weight after the third fall. This is point E, $^{-}4$. I move 1 unit to the right, which is the location of the weight after it rises a third time. The weight will be at $^{-}3$ cm after the third rise.

Name ______________________ Date __________

Integer Cubes

Suppose you have a number cube labeled 1–6 and a number cube labeled $^{-}1$–$^{-}6$. You toss the number cubes at the same time and add the integers shown.

Complete the table to show all the possible outcomes by adding the number in the left column to the number in the top row.

Possible Outcomes						
	1	2	3	4	5	6
$^{-}1$						
$^{-}2$						
$^{-}3$						
$^{-}4$						
$^{-}5$						
$^{-}6$						

1. What is the probability that the sum is zero? ______________________

2. **Explain** What is the probability that the sum is a negative integer? Explain how you found the answer.

____

____

3. **Infer** Suppose the number cubes were changed to have 8 sides instead of 6. They are labeled 1–8 and $^{-}1$–$^{-}8$. Without making a new table, explain how you could find the probability that the sum is zero.

____

____

4. Without making a new table, how could you find the probability that the sum is negative? positive?

____

____

Extend It

How could you change the 6-sided number cubes so the probability that the sum is negative would be greater than the probability that the sum is positive? On a separate sheet of paper, explain your answer.

Teacher Notes

Extend: Integer Cubes

Objective Use number cubes to explore integers and probability.

Using the Extend (Activities to use after Lesson 3)

In this activity, students combine the skills of adding integers and calculating probabilities by using number cubes with positive and negative integers. The critical thinking questions encourage students to use integer addition and extend this skill to a scenario with an 8-sided number polyhedron. In the Extend It students change the numbers on the number cubes to produce different outcomes.

Math Journal You may wish to have students use their *Math Journals* for the Extend It.

Going Beyond Have students calculate probabilities using two integer number polyhedrons with each polyhedron having a different number of sides.

Solutions

Possible Outcomes						
	1	2	3	4	5	6
$^-1$	**0**	**1**	**2**	**3**	**4**	**5**
$^-2$	**$^-1$**	**0**	**1**	**2**	**3**	**4**
$^-3$	**$^-2$**	**$^-1$**	**0**	**1**	**2**	**3**
$^-4$	**$^-3$**	**$^-2$**	**$^-1$**	**0**	**1**	**2**
$^-5$	**$^-4$**	**$^-3$**	**$^-2$**	**$^-1$**	**0**	**1**
$^-6$	**$^-5$**	**$^-4$**	**$^-3$**	**$^-2$**	**$^-1$**	**0**

1. $\frac{1}{6}$

2. $\frac{15}{36}$; *Answers may vary. Sample:* I counted the total number of outcomes, 36. Then I counted the number of outcomes with a negative integer, 15. The probability is $\frac{15}{36}$.

3. *Answers may vary. Sample:* In the table for the 6-sided cube, the number of zeros is equal to the number of sides on the number cube, which is 6. So, there will be 8 zeros for an 8-sided polyhedron. The probability is $\frac{8}{64}$, or $\frac{1}{8}$.

4. *Answers may vary. Sample:* There are 64 outcomes. 8 of the outcomes are zero. $64 - 8 = 56$. Half of the remaining outcomes are positive and half are negative. $56 \div 2 = 28$. The probability that the sum is positive or negative is the same: $\frac{28}{64}$, or $\frac{7}{16}$.

Extend It *Answers may vary. Sample:* You could change a number on the 1–6 number cube to a negative number.

Name ______________________ Date __________

Integer Puzzles

In this puzzle activity, your task is to fit each group of counting numbers, operations, and signs into the boxes to make the equation true. You can use each number, operation, or sign only as many times as it is given. The first equation has been done for you.

	Equation	Numbers	Operations	Signs
	$^{-}5 - {}^{-}1 + {}^{+}3 = {}^{-}1$	3 5 1	+ −	+ − −
1.	□□ □ □□ □ □□ $= {}^{-}2$	4 1 3	+ +	+ − −
2.	□□ □ □□ □ □□ $= {}^{+}8$	4 2 6	+ −	+ − −
3.	□□ □ □□ □ □□ □ □□ $= {}^{-}6$	5 1 2 4	+ − −	+ + − −
4.	□□ □ □□ □ □□ □ □□ $= 0$	7 6 2 3	+ + −	+ − − −

5. Explain How did you decide where to place each item in the boxes in Exercise 1?

____

____

Connect It

In Exercise 1, suppose all the integers to the left of the equal sign were changed to their opposites. How does the integer to the right of the equal sign change? On a separate sheet of paper, explain your answer.

Teacher Notes

Connect: Integer Puzzles

Objective Use integer addition and subtraction to solve a puzzle.

Using the Connect (Activities to use after Lesson 5)

Students already have learned how to add and subtract integers. In this activity, students use these skills and logical reasoning to solve puzzles. The critical thinking question asks students to describe the strategies they used. The Connect It asks students to explain the effect of opposites on the puzzle.

Math Journal You may wish to have students use their *Math Journals* for the Connect It.

Going Beyond Have students create similar puzzles using inequalities with *greater than* and *less than* symbols.

Solutions

Order of integers may vary in Exercises 1–4. Samples:

1. $^{-}1 + {}^{-}4 + {}^{+}3 = {}^{-}2$
2. $^{+}6 + {}^{-}2 - {}^{-}4 = {}^{+}8$
3. $^{-}5 - {}^{-}2 + {}^{+}1 - {}^{+}4 = {}^{-}6$
4. $^{-}3 + {}^{-}6 - {}^{-}7 + {}^{+}2 = 0$
5. *Answers may vary. Sample:* I knew that the absolute value of 1 plus 4 equals 5. I knew that subtracting 3 would give me 2. Since I was looking for a $^{-}2$, I made the 1 and 4 negative and the 3 positive. $^{-}1 + {}^{-}4 + {}^{+}3 = {}^{-}2$.

Connect It *Answers may vary. Sample:* The integer on the right side of the equal sign changes to its opposite: $^{-}2$ changes to $^{+}2$.

Name ______________________ Date ____________

Using Ordered Pairs in the Coordinate Plane

Mr. Schafer is taking his class on a nature walk. He has made a map and "mathematical walking tour directions" for the morning.

Directions:

- Start at the Welcome Center.
- Stop 1: Walk to the point (3, 1).
- Stop 2: Walk north 2 units.
- Stop 3: Walk west 4 units.
- Stop 4: Walk to ($^-1$, $^-3$)
- Stop 5: Walk east 1 unit and north 3 units.

Mr. Schafer's Map

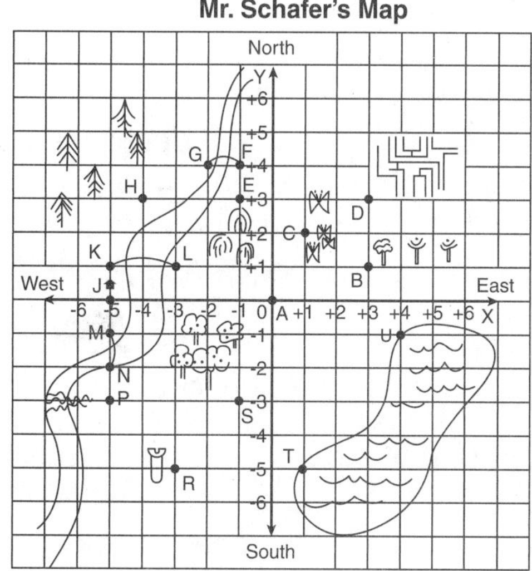

Legend	
A	Welcome Center
B	Rose Garden
C	Butterfly Garden
D	Hedge Maze
E	Haystacks
F,G	Foot Bridge
H	Owls
J	Log Cabin
K,L	Foot Bridge
M,N	Foot Bridge
P	Waterfall
R	Tower
S	Apple Orchard
T	Turtles
U	Ducks

1. List the sights that the students saw at each stop on the walking tour. Did they see any turtles? How do you know?

____

2. Jack gave Stephanie the following walking directions to see the owls.

- Start at the Welcome Center.
- Go to ($^-1$, 3).
- Walk west 3 units, and you will see the owls.

Do you think that Jack's directions are good directions? Why or why not?

____

3. **Create** On a separate sheet of paper, design a walking tour for the afternoon that includes sights in each of the four quadrants.

Explore It

Create a tour that starts and finishes at the Welcome Center, is exactly 28 units long, and stops at the butterfly garden, the log cabin, the tower, and the turtles. Use the map and coordinates to explain how you calculated the distance.

Teacher Notes

Explore: Using Ordered Pairs in the Coordinate Plane

Objective Graph and read ordered pairs in all four quadrants of the coordinate plane.

Using the Explore (Activities to use after Lesson 1)

In this activity, students use ordered pairs to follow a path. They are encouraged to plot a new path through all four quadrants by giving coordinates. The Explore It challenges students to calculate distances by adding and subtracting *x*- and *y*-coordinates.

Math Journal You may wish to have students use their *Math Journals* to answer the Explore It question.

Going Beyond Encourage students to create their own map of a park. Have them decide what elements will be in the park, what their coordinates will be, and create a walking path.

Solutions

1. Stop 1: Rose Garden, Stop 2: Hedge Maze, Stop 3: Haystacks, Stop 4: Apple Orchard, Stop 5: Welcome Center. *Answers may vary. Sample:* No. They did not see any turtles. They did not walk into the quadrant where the turtles are located.
2. *Answers may vary. Sample:* No. Jack's directions are not good directions. They cross the river at a point where there is no footbridge.
3. *Answers may vary. Check students' work.*

Explore It *Answers may vary. Sample:* One possible tour starts and ends at the Welcome Center and follows this path: (0, 0), (1, 0), (1, 2), ($^-$2, 2), ($^-$2, 1), ($^-$3, 1), ($^-$5, 1), ($^-$5, 0), ($^-$5, $^-$1), ($^-$5, $^-$2), ($^-$3, $^-$2), ($^-$3, $^-$5), (1, $^-$5), (1, 0), (0, 0). You can find the distance by counting the difference between the *y*-coordinates as you move vertically or the *x*-coordinates as you move horizontally.

Name ______________________ Date __________

Graphing Linear Functions

You can select your favorite songs and create your own CD. You can also buy songs to download from the Internet. Analyze the costs to decide which option is the least expensive for you.

Create Your Own CD	**Download Individual Songs**
Cost is 50¢ per song plus an additional $6 for making and shipping the CD.	Cost is $1 per song.

Let x = number of songs that you buy. Let y = total cost.

1. Substitute each value of x into the functions to find the value of y.

2. Use the coordinate grid shown below to graph all of the points for each function. Use a different color for each function. Use the same colors to connect the points for each function.

Create Your Own CD	
$y = 0.50x + 6$	
x	y
2	
4	
6	
8	
10	
12	
14	

Download Songs	
$y = 1x$	
x	y
2	
4	
6	
8	
10	
12	
14	

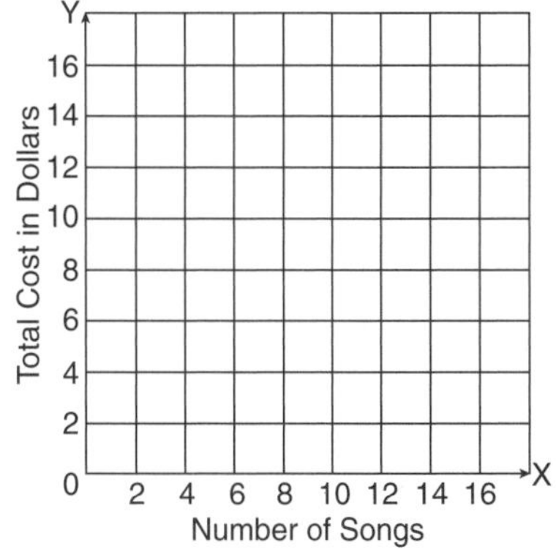

3. **Infer** At what coordinates do the lines intersect? Explain in terms of the number of songs and the total cost what happens when the two lines intersect.

____

Extend It

If you only want to buy 8 songs, would you recommend creating your own CD or downloading the songs? What if you want to buy 14 songs? Use the graph and the data to support your answers.

Teacher Notes

Extend: Graphing Linear Functions

Objective Use graphs of linear functions to predict solutions.
Materials colored pencils

Using the Extend (Activities to use after Lesson 3)

In this activity, students use graphs and linear functions to help them make consumer decisions. Critical thinking questions prompt students to analyze graphs in greater detail, particularly where the lines intersect. The Extend It challenges students to use the graph to decide under what circumstances they might choose one plan over another.

Math Journal You may wish to have students use their *Math Journals* to answer the Extend It question.

Going Beyond Encourage students to think about when they would recommend creating a CD versus downloading individual songs. Challenge them to think about the limitations of each plan.

Solutions

1.

$y = 0.50x + 6$	
x	y
2	7
4	8
6	9
8	10
10	11
12	12
14	13

$y = 1x$	
x	y
2	2
4	4
6	6
8	8
10	10
12	12
14	14

2.

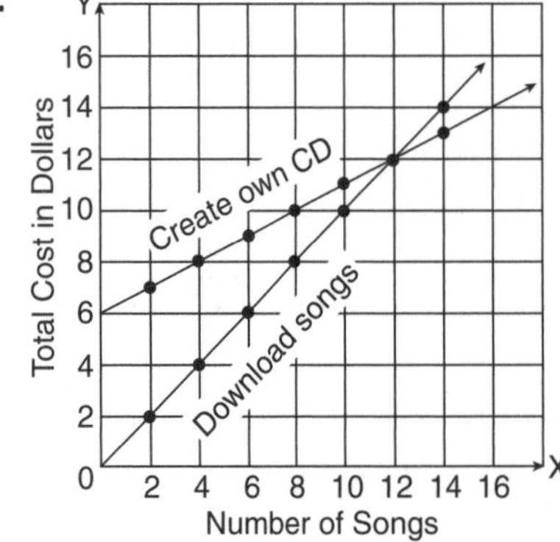

3. The lines intersect at (12, 12). *Answers may vary. Sample:* This means that when you buy 12 songs using either plan, the cost is $12.

Extend It *Answers may vary. Sample:* If I want to buy 8 songs, I would download the songs because the cost is only $8. It would cost $10 to create my own CD. If I want to buy 14 songs I would create my own CD because it would be less expensive than downloading the songs. It would cost $13, which is less than $14.

Name ______________________________ Date ____________

Transformations in the Coordinate Plane

Mark is trying to solve a new puzzle. He must move the triangle from Quadrant I, through each quadrant in order from I to IV, to overlay the triangle in Quadrant IV. He must use the following moves, but they can be used in any order.

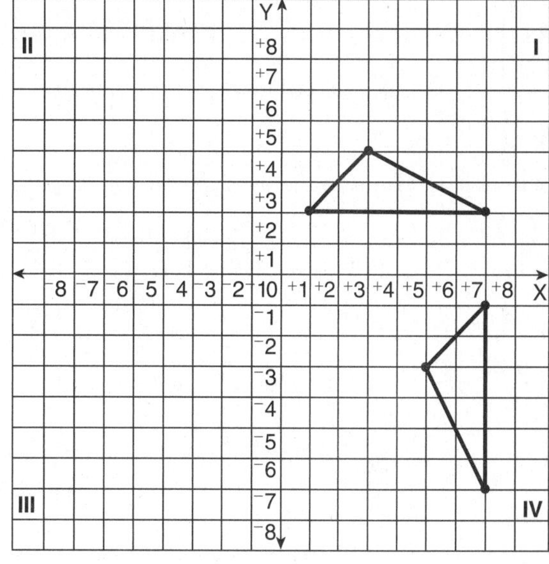

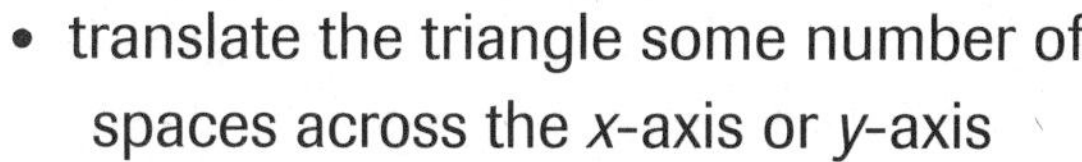

- translate the triangle some number of spaces across the *x*-axis or *y*-axis
- rotate the triangle a $\frac{1}{4}$ turn counterclockwise around (0, 0)
- reflect the triangle over the *x*-axis or *y*-axis

1. Help Mark solve the puzzle. Record each transformation you make.

____

____

2. His sister Sarah thinks that there is more than one way to solve the puzzle. Is she correct? Explain your answer. ______________________

____

3. **Predict** Is the order of the transformations important? How do you know? ______________________

____

Connect It

Can you solve this puzzle using only two of the transformations? Explain why or why not.

Teacher Notes

Connect: Transformations in the Coordinate Plane

Objective Identify and describe transformations in a coordinate plane.

Using the Connect (Activities to use after Lesson 5)

In this activity, students are challenged to use transformations to solve a geometric puzzle in the coordinate plane. Students must use their knowledge of transformations to find all of the possible solutions to the puzzle. The Connect It question challenges students to look at alternate solutions to the puzzle.

Math Journal You may wish to have students use their *Math Journals* to answer the Connect It question.

Going Beyond Have students create their own transformation puzzles with solutions. Encourage them to think about the rules they will create for solving the puzzle.

Solutions

1. *Answers may vary. Samples:*
   - Reflect over the y-axis, $(^-1, 2)$ $(^-3, 4)$ $(^-7, 2)$. Translate down 9, $(^-1, ^-7)$ $(^-3, ^-5)$ $(^-7, ^-7)$. Rotate 90° around (0, 0).
   - Reflect over the y-axis, $(^-1, 2)$ $(^-3, 4)$ $(^-7, 2)$. Rotate 90° around (0, 0), $(^-2, ^-1)$ $(^-4, ^-3)$ $(^-2, ^-7)$. Translate right 9.
   - Rotate 90° around (0, 0), $(^-2, 1)$ $(^-4, 3)$ $(^-2, 7)$. Reflect over the x-axis, $(^-2, ^-1)$ $(^-4, ^-3)$ $(^-2, ^-7)$. Translate right 9.
2. *Answers may vary. Sample:* Yes. There is more than one way to solve the puzzle. You can change the order of the moves.
3. *Answers may vary. Sample:* Yes. The order of transformations is important. If you try to translate the triangle first, you cannot solve the puzzle.

Connect It *Answers may vary. Sample:* No. You cannot solve the puzzle with only two transformations. The combinations of rotate/translate, rotate/reflect, translate/reflect do not end with the triangle in Quadrant IV.

Additional Answers

Chapter 20, Connect, p. 120

Connect It *Answers may vary. Sample:* No. This doesn't account for the tornadoes' locations, so it doesn't help predict *where* they will occur. It would be more accurate if the data were divided by state or region. *Or* No. This data is only for 5 years, and that's not a large enough sample. For example, one extremely high January record changes the January average from 18 to 57. Many more years of data would make the predictions more accurate.